Macmillan McGraw-Hill

Math Connects 4

Homework Practice Workbook

Macmillan/McGraw-Hill

TO THE STUDENT This *Homework Practice Workbook* gives you additional examples and problems for the concept exercises in each lesson. The exercises are designed to help you study mathematics by reinforcing important skills needed to succeed in the everyday world. The materials are organized by chapter and lesson, with one Homework Practice worksheet for every lesson in *Math Connects, Grade 4*.

Always keep your workbook handy. Along with you textbook, daily homework, and class notes, the completed *Homework Practice Workbook* can help you in reviewing for quizzes and tests.

TO THE TEACHER These worksheets are the same ones found in the Chapter Resource Masters for *Math Connects, Grade 4*. The answers to these worksheets are available at the end of each Chapter Resource Masters booklet.

The McGraw·Hill Companies

 Macmillan/McGraw-Hill

Copyright © by the McGraw-Hill Companies, Inc. All rights reserved. Except as permitted under the United States Copyright Act, no part of this publication may be reproduced or distributed in any form or by any means, or stored in a database or retrieval system, without prior written permission of the publisher.

Send all inquiries to:
Macmillan/McGraw-Hill
8787 Orion Place
Columbus, OH 43240

ISBN: 978-0-02-107298-9
MHID: 0-02-107298-1

Homework Practice Workbook, Grade 4

Printed in the United States of America.

2 3 4 5 6 7 8 9 10   021   14 13 12 11 10 09 08

CONTENTS

Chapter 1 Use Place Value to Represent Whole Numbers
- 1-1 Place Value Through Hundred Thousands . . 1
- 1-2 Place Value Through Millions 2
- 1-3 Problem-Solving Strategy: The Four-Step Plan 3
- 1-4 Compare Whole Numbers 4
- 1-5 Order Whole Numbers 5
- 1-6 Round Whole Numbers 6
- 1-7 Problem-Solving Investigation: Choose a Strategy 7

Chapter 2 Solve Addition and Subtraction Problems
- 2-1 Algebra: Addition Properties and Subtraction Rules 8
- 2-2 Estimate Sums and Differences 9
- 2-3 Problem-Solving Skill: Estimate or Exact Answer 10
- 2-4 Add Whole Numbers 11
- 2-5 Subtract Whole Numbers 12
- 2-6 Problem-Solving Investigation: Choose a Strategy 13
- 2-7 Subtract Across Zeros 14

Chapter 3 Organize, Display, and Interpret Data
- 3-1 Collect and Organize Data 15
- 3-2 Find Mode, Median, and Outliers 16
- 3-3 Problem-Solving Strategy: Make a Table 17
- 3-4 Line Plots 18
- 3-5 Bar Graphs 19
- 3-6 Bar and Double Bar Graphs 20
- 3-7 Problem-Solving Investigation: Choose a Strategy 21
- 3-8 Determine Possible Outcomes 22
- 3-9 Probability 23

Chapter 4 Apply Multiplication and Division Facts
- 4-1 Relate Multiplication and Division 24
- 4-2 Algebra: Multiplication Properties and Division Rules 25
- 4-3 Multiply and Divide Facts Through 5 26
- 4-4 Problem-Solving Skill: Choose an Operation 27
- 4-5 Multiply and Divide Facts Through 10 28
- 4-6 Multiply with 11 and 12 29
- 4-7 Problem-Solving Investigation: Choose a Strategy 30
- 4-8 Algebra: Multiply Three Numbers 31
- 4-9 Factors and Multiples 32

Chapter 5 Describe Algebraic Patterns
- 5-1 Addition and Subtraction Expressions 33
- 5-2 Solve Equations 34
- 5-3 Problem-Solving Skill: Extra or Missing Information 35
- 5-4 Identify, Describe, and Extend Patterns . . . 36
- 5-5 Function Tables: Find a Rule (+,-) 37
- 5-6 Multiplication and Division Expressions 38
- 5-7 Problem-Solving Investigation: Choose a Strategy 39
- 5-8 Function Tables: Find a Rule (×, ÷) 40

Chapter 6 Multiply by One-Digit Numbers
- 6-1 Multiples of 10, 100 and 1,000 41
- 6-2 Problem-Solving Skill: Reasonable Answers 42
- 6-3 Use Rounding to Estimate Products 43
- 6-4 Multiply Two-Digit Numbers 44
- 6-5 Problem-Solving Investigation: Choose a Strategy 45
- 6-6 Multiply Multi-Digit Numbers 46
- 6-7 Multiply Across Zeros 47

Chapter 7 Multiply by Two-Digit Numbers
- 7-1 Multiply by Tens 48
- 7-2 Estimate Products 49
- 7-3 Problem-Solving Strategy: Act It Out 50
- 7-4 Multiply Two-Digit Numbers 51
- 7-5 Multiply Three-Digit Numbers by Two-Digit Numbers 52
- 7-6 Problem-Solving Investigation: Choose a Strategy 53
- 7-7 Multiply Greater Numbers 54

Chapter 8 Divide by One-Digit Numbers
- 8-1 Division with Remainders 55
- 8-2 Divide Multiples of 10, 100 and 1,000 56
- 8-3 Problem-Solving Strategy: Guess and Check 57
- 8-4 Estimate Quotients 58
- 8-5 Two-Digit Quotients 59
- 8-6 Problem-Solving Investigation: Choose a Strategy 60
- 8-7 Three-Digit Quotients 61
- 8-8 Quotients with Zeros 62
- 8-9 Divide Greater Numbers 63

Chapter 9 Identify and Describe Geometric Figures
- 9-1 Three-Dimensional Figures 64
- 9-2 Two-Dimensional Figures 65
- 9-3 Problem-Solving Strategy: Look for a Pattern 66
- 9-4 Angles............................. 67
- 9-5 Triangles........................... 68
- 9-6 Quadrilaterals....................... 69
- 9-7 Problem-Solving Investigation: Choose a Strategy................... 70

Chapter 10 Understand and Develop Spatial Reasoning
- 10-1 Locate Points on a Number Line 71
- 10-2 Lines, Line Segments, and Rays 72
- 10-3 Problem-Solving Strategy: Make an Organized List 73
- 10-4 Find Points on a Grid................. 74
- 10-5 Rotations, Reflections, and Translations 75
- 10-6 Problem-Solving Investigation: Choose a Strategy................... 76
- 10-7 Congruent Figures................... 77
- 10-8 Symmetry......................... 78

Chapter 11 Measure Length, Area, and Temperature
- 11-1 Customary Units of Length............ 79
- 11-2 Convert Customary Units of Length...... 80
- 11-3 Problem-Solving Strategy: Solve a Simpler Problem 81
- 11-4 Metric Units of Length................ 82
- 11-5 Measure Perimeters 83
- 11-6 Measure Areas 84
- 11-7 Problem-Solving Investigation: Choose a Strategy................... 85
- 11-8 Measure Temperatures............... 86

Chapter 12 Measure Capacity, Weight, and Volume
- 12-1 Customary Units of Capacity 87
- 12-2 Convert Customary Units of Capacity 88
- 12-3 Metric Units of Capacity 89
- 12-4 Customary Units of Weights........... 90
- 12-5 Problem-Solving Strategy: Use Logical Reasoning 91
- 12-6 Convert Customary Units of Weight...... 92
- 12-7 Metric Units of Mass 93
- 12-8 Estimate and Measure Volumes 94
- 12-9 Problem-Solving Investigation: Choose a Strategy................... 95
- 12-10 Elapsed Time....................... 96

Chapter 13 Describe and Compare Fractions
- 13-1 Parts of a Whole 97
- 13-2 Parts of a Set....................... 98
- 13-3 Problem-Solving Strategy: Draw a Picture 99
- 13-4 Equivalent Fractions 100
- 13-5 Compare and Order Fractions 101
- 13-6 Mixed Numbers 102
- 13-7 Problem-Solving Investigation: Choose a Strategy.................. 103

Chapter 14 Use Place Value to Represent Decimals
- 14-1 Tenths and Hundredths 104
- 14-2 Relate Mixed Numbers and Decimals 105
- 14-3 Problem-Solving Strategy: Make a Model 106
- 14-4 Locate Fraction and Decimals on a Number Line 107
- 14-5 Compare and Order Decimals 108
- 14-6 Problem-Solving Investigation: Choose a Strategy.................. 109
- 14-7 Fraction and Decimal Equivalents 110
- 14-8 Decimals, Fractions, and Mixed Numbers 111

Chapter 15 Add and Subtract Decimals
- 15-1 Round Decimals 112
- 15-2 Estimate Decimal Sums and Differences........................ 113
- 15-3 Problem-Solving Strategy: Work Backward 114
- 15-4 Add Decimals...................... 115
- 15-5 Problem-Solving Investigation: Choose a Strategy.................. 116
- 15-6 Subtract Decimals 117

1-1

Name _____

Homework Practice

Place Value Through Hundred Thousands

Write each number in standard form.

1. three hundred twenty-six thousand, four hundred fifty-one.
   _____

2. one hundred forty-five thousand, two hundred thirty-seven.
   _____

Write each number in word form and expanded form.

3. 87,192
   _____
   _____

4. 413,750
   _____
   _____

Complete the expanded form.

5. 91,765 = 90,000 + _____ + 700 + _____ + 5

6. 798,054 = 700,000 = _____ + 8,000 + _____ + 4

Write the value of each underlined digit.

7. 645,<u>8</u>02 _____

8. 27<u>1</u>,385 _____

Spiral Review

Divide.

9. 550 ÷ 2 _____

10. 616 ÷ 2 _____

11. 333 ÷ 3 _____

12. 725 ÷ 5 _____

13. 447 ÷ 4 _____

14. 860 ÷ 6 _____

15. 3)̅6̅3̅2̅ _____

16. 5)̅4̅6̅0̅ _____

17. 3)̅7̅4̅0̅ _____

18. 4)̅9̅8̅5̅ _____

19. 3)̅6̅2̅2̅ _____

20. 4)̅2̅7̅5̅ _____

1-2 Homework Practice

Name _____

Place Value Through Millions

Write each number in standard form.

1. four hundred thirty-two million, five hundred eighty-six thousand, six hundred twelve. _____

2. nine hundred fifty-seven million, two hundred four thousand, three hundred eighty-one. _____

Write each number in word form and expanded form.

3. 103,721,495

_____
_____
_____
_____

4. 682,364,518

_____
_____
_____
_____

Write the value of each underlined digit.

5. 5_6_1,754,908 _____ 6. 498,749,013 _____

7. _7_,020,154 _____ 8. _3_98,216,045 _____

Spiral Review

Write the number in standard form. (Lesson 1-1)

9. two hundred forty-three thousand, seven hundred eighteen
_____

10. six hundred ninety-five thousand, eighty-seven _____

Complete the expanded form.

11. 198,045 = 100,000 + 90,000 + _____ + 40 + _____

12. 982,105 = 900,000 + _____ + 2,000 + _____ + 5

Grade 4 2 Chapter 1

Name _____

1-3 Homework Practice

Problem-Solving Strategy

Solve. Use the four-step plan.

1. Luis can ride his bike to school three different ways. When he goes with Christina, it takes 22 minutes. When he goes with Devin, it takes 17 minutes. When he goes by himself, it takes 12 minutes. How much faster can Luis get to school when he rides by himself than with Christina?

   _____

2. Marissa wants to buy her brother a present. The store has a $10 soccer ball, a $9 baseball bat, an $18 baseball glove, a $13 tennis racket, and a $21 helmet. If Marissa has $15, which presents could she buy?

   _____

3. Inez can carry 2 bags of groceries into her home with each trip from the car. Her brother can carry the same amount. How many trips will it take them to carry 27 bags of groceries?

   _____

4. Carlos wants to go to Happy Land Park with 4 friends at the end of summer. Tickets are $18 for children. How much will it cost for Carlos and his friends to go to Happy Land Park?

   _____

Spiral Review

Write each number in standard form. (Lesson 1-2)

5. five hundred eighty-seven million, one hundred forty-two thousand, eight hundred sixty-six

   _____

6. one hundred twenty million, five hundred seventy-four thousand, two hundred seventy-five

   _____

Write the value of each underlined digit.

7. 3<u>1</u>6,113,276 _____   8. 67,<u>5</u>12,327 _____

1-4

Name _____

Homework Practice

Compare Whole Numbers

Compare. Use >, <, or =.

1. 1,347 ◯ 1,317
2. 5,781 ◯ 5,872
3. 8,091 ◯ 8,901
4. 11,654 ◯ 1,654
5. 77,215 ◯ 77,215
6. 97,604 ◯ 96,407
7. 111,280 ◯ 112,800
8. 234,582 ◯ 23,458
9. 366,438 ◯ 366,843
10. 672,809 ◯ 672,809
11. 702,593 ◯ 702,359
12. 894,710 ◯ 89,470
13. 1,436,721 ◯ 1,346,721
14. 23,086,543 ◯ 23,806,543
15. 527,308,516 ◯ 523,708,500
16. fifty-two thousand, four hundred sixty-seven ◯ 502,467
17. 800,000 + 60,000 + 400 + 60 + 2 ◯ 97,642
18. four million, two hundred twelve thousand, thirty-two ◯ 4,000,000 + 9,000 + 50 + 9
19. 6,821,054 ◯ sixteen million, five hundred twelve thousand, eight hundred fourteen

Spiral Review

Solve. Use the four-step plan. (Lesson 1-3)

20. Sierra wants to climb the tallest mountain on each continent. She has already climbed the third tallest, Mt. McKinley (20,321 ft.) She wants to try a taller one next. Which of these is taller than Mt. McKinley: Kilimanjaro (19,337 ft.) or Aconcagua (22,841 ft.)?

21. Jake delivers 1,234 newspapers a week. Miranda delivers 1,407 newspapers a week. Who delivers more newspapers?

Name _____

1-5 Homework Practice

Order Whole Numbers

Order the numbers from greatest to least.

1. 5,827; 5,628; 5,835; 5,725

2. 17,472; 18,451; 19,629; 17,784

3. 34,893; 37,230; 29,167; 38,173

4. 273,280; 267,902; 275,784; 270,562

5. 478,024; 478,165; 475,907; 477,281

Solve.

6. Christine is writing a report about the world's largest animals. Order these animals by weight from greatest to least to help her decide which animals to write about first.
   Blue whale: 418,878 lbs   African elephant: 11,023 lbs
   White rhinoceros: 4,850 lbs   Indian elephant: 8,818 lbs

7. Nicole wants to learn more about the islands of the world. Order these islands from greatest to least.
   Borneo 287,300 mi   Madagascar 227,000 mi
   New Guinea 309,000 mi   Greenland 839,999 mi

Spiral Review

Compare. Use >, <, or =.

8. 907,654 ◯ 987,421   9. 1,235,903 ◯ 1,237,903

Grade 4   5   Chapter 1

1-6

Name _____

Homework Practice

Round Whole Numbers

Round each number to the given place-value position.

1. 623; ten _____
2. 435; ten _____
3. 581; hundred _____
4. 870; hundred _____
5. 1,302; hundred _____
6. 1,447; hundred _____
7. 2,398; thousand _____
8. 4,628; thousand _____
9. 23,876; thousand _____
10. 31,098; thousand _____
11. 44,872; ten thousand _____
12. 65,281; ten thousand _____
13. 124,830; ten thousand _____
14. 237,524; hundred thousand _____
15. 497,320; hundred thousand _____
16. 1,567,438; hundred thousand _____
17. 2,802,746; hundred thousand _____
18. 3,458,321; million _____
19. 4,872,018; million _____
20. 6,873,652; thousand _____

Solve.

21. There are 572 beans in the jar. Carolina guesses there are 600 beans in the jar. Steven estimates there are 500 beans in the jar. Rounding to the hundred, who estimated correctly?

_____

Order from greatest to least. (Lesson 1-5)

22. 564; 623; 276

_____

23. 3,560; 3,542; 3,498; 3,589

_____

24. 64,890; 65,032; 64,217; 64,578

_____

25. 213,093; 212,764; 213,570; 213,435

_____

Name _____

1-7 Homework Practice

Problem-Solving Investigation: Choose a Strategy

Use any strategy shown below to solve. Tell which one you used.

- Use the four-step plan
- Draw a picture
- Look for a pattern
- Make a table

1. Alexis and Tyler are getting a dog. They like labradors, golden retrievers, and dalmatians. Their mother said they can get the smallest dog. The average labrador is 70 pounds. The average golden retriever is 65 pounds. The average dalmatian is 55 pounds. Which dog will Alexis and Tyler get?

   _____

2. Marisol sells candy bars to raise money for her softball team. Each day she sells more. The first day she sells 5. The second day she sells 6. The third day she sells 8. The fourth day she sells 11. The fifth day she sells 15. The sixth day she sells 20. How many will she sell on the tenth day? _____

3. Erica was searching for her sunglasses. She walked 2 blocks north, 3 blocks south, 4 blocks east, and 3 blocks west. How many blocks did she walk? How far is Erica from where she began her search?

   _____

   _____

4. Paige and her 3 friends want to go to the movies on Saturday. If tickets are $6 each, how much will it cost for all 4 friends to go to the movies? _____

Spiral Review

Round each number to the given place-value position. (Lesson 1-6)

5. 4,563; hundred _____
6. 7,412; hundred _____
7. 12,763; thousand _____
8. 67,924; ten thousand _____
9. 137,654; ten thousand _____
10. 472,917; hundred thousand _____
11. 2,348,915; million _____
12. 4,712,634; million _____

Grade 4

2-1

Name _____

Homework Practice

Algebra: Addition Properties and Subtraction Rules

Complete each number sentence. Identify the property or rule used.

1. $85 + 0 =$ _____
   _____

2. $96 + 13 = 13 +$ _____
   _____

3. _____ $- 0 = 37$
   _____

4. $(15 + 23) + 7 = 15 + ($_____$+ 7)$
   _____

5. $67 + 29 + 31 = 29 + 31 +$ _____
   _____

6. $452 -$ _____ $= 452$
   _____

Spiral Review

Round each number to the given place-value position.

7. 582; ten _____

8. 391; hundred _____

9. 749; ten _____

10. 248; ten _____

11. 8,763; thousand _____

12. 1,421; hundred _____

13. 5,717; thousand _____

14. 38,954; thousand _____

15. 1,579; hundred _____

16. 1,337; ten _____

17. 40,397; thousand _____

18. 58,852; hundred _____

2-2

Name _____

Homework Practice

Estimate Sums and Differences

Round to the nearest hundred.

1. 327
   + 548 _____

2. $739
   + $461 _____

3. 8,752
   − 3,269 _____

4. 9,399
   − 3,431 _____

Round to the nearest thousand.

5. $5,486
   + $8,602 _____

6. 16,807
   + 7,279 _____

7. 38,295
   − 11,690 _____

8. $95,438
   − $62,804 _____

The table shows the driving distances between some major U.S. cities.

New York City, NY, to Chicago, IL	800 miles
Chicago, IL, to Los Angeles, CA	2,090 miles

9. David is planning a trip over summer vacation. About how many miles will his family drive if they go from New York City to Chicago and then to Los Angeles? Round your answer to the nearest hundred.

_____

Spiral Review

Complete each number sentence. Identify the property or rule shown. (Lesson 2-1)

10. 25 − _____ = 0

    _____

12. 54 + _____ = 54

    _____

11. 9 + 3 + 7 = 7 + 9 + _____

    _____

13. (12 + _____) + 11 = 12 + (7 + 11)

    _____

Grade 4   9   Chapter 2

Name _____

2-3 Homework Practice

Problem-Solving Skill: Estimate or Exact Answer

Tell whether an estimate or an exact answer is needed. Then solve.

1. Brandi is going to her friend's house after her soccer game. It takes her 18 minutes to shower and change clothes. Then it takes her 31 minutes to get to her friend's house. If her game is over at 2:00 p.m., what time will she arrive at her friend's house?

   _____

2. Monica and her family went to the movies on Saturday. Adult tickets cost $7 and children's tickets cost $4. How much did they spend if they bought two adult tickets and one children's ticket?

   _____

3. A minor league baseball team wanted to determine if they set a new attendance record for a weekend. The first game had an attendance of 13,209 people. The second game had an attendance of 12,489 people. What was the combined attendance for both games?

   _____

 (Lesson 2-2)

Round to the nearest hundred.

4. 886 − 174 = _____

5. 612 + 914 = _____

6. 826 − 590 = _____

Round to the nearest thousand.

7. 7,378 − 5,903 = _____

8. 22,358 − 14,699 = _____

9. 8,723 − 4,235 = _____

10. 2,799 + 11,089 = _____

Grade 4   10   Chapter 2

2-4

Name _____

Homework Practice

Add Whole Numbers

Find each sum. Check your work by estimating.

1. 651
  + 274

2. 5,239
  + 2,794

3. $727
  + 657

4. 169,748
  + 355,470

5. 219
  + 566

6. 4,189
  + 5,432

Tell whether an estimate or an exact answer is needed. Then solve. (Lesson 2-3)

7. John and his father are building a birdhouse. They need one 12-inch long piece of wood, one 17-inch long piece of wood, and one 9-inch long piece of wood. How many inches of wood do John and his father need to buy?

   _____

8. Maria and her mom spent $12 for tickets to a soccer game. They also spent $7 on food and $23 on souvenirs. How much did they spend?

   _____

9. John wants to build a model car. The kit for the car costs $19, glue costs $8, and paint costs $11. How much money does he need to build the car?

   _____

2-5

Name _____

Homework Practice

Subtract Whole Numbers

Subtract. Use addition or estimation to check.

1. 940
   − 271

2. $6,148
   − $1,575

3. $821
   − $569

4. 644
   − 361

5. 9,516
   − 7,228

6. 33,539
   − 31,649

7. $985 − $527 = n _____

8. 6,637 − 2,846 = n _____

Solve.

9. John Stennis was a senator from Mississippi. He was first elected to the U.S. Senate in 1947. He served in the Senate until 1989. How long was he a senator? _____

Spiral Review

Find each sum. (Lesson 2-4)

10. 651
    + 274

11. 9,446
    + 4,187

12. 366
    + 749

13. $3,912
    + $2,199

14. 2,358
    + 965

15. 41,927
    +53,157

Grade 4   12   Chapter 2

Name _____

2-6 Homework Practice

Problem-Solving Investigation: Choose a Strategy

Use the four-step plan, estimation, or an exact answer to solve each problem.

1. Thomas has 324 coins in his coin collection. Mia has 297 in her coin collection. About how many do they have together?

   _____

2. Mrs. Ramirez bought sweaters for her children. She spent $23, $28, and $34 on the sweaters. About how much did she spend on sweaters?

   _____

3. Maya had $45. She bought a skirt for $25 and a book for $14. How much money does she have left?

   _____

4. Fernando's class has 25 students in it. Will's class has 5 more than Fernando's. How many students does Will's class have?

   _____

5. Niko has bought 7 pairs of socks in the last year. If each pair of socks costs about $4, how much has he spent?

   _____

Find each difference. Use addition or estimation to check. (Lesson 2-5)

6. 780 − 456 _____

7. $459 − $339 _____

8. 459 − 83 _____

9. 1,405 − 222 _____

10. $698 − $241 _____

Name _____

2-7 Homework Practice

Subtract Across Zeros

Subtract. Use addition to check.

1.   500
   − 360
   _____

2.   800
   − 279
   _____

3. $1,300
   − $ 637
   _____

4.   1,100
   −   628
   _____

5.   4,000
   − 1,731
   _____

6.   3,300
   − 1,892
   _____

7.   8,000
   − 6,313
   _____

8.   3,000
   − 1,811
   _____

9. $14,000
   − $10,892
   _____

10.   9,000
    − 5,281
    _____

Spiral Review

Tell whether an estimate or exact answer is needed. Then solve.
(Lesson 2-6)

11. The flowers cost $9, the clay pot costs $29, and the bag of soil costs $7. How much does it cost to plant the flowers in all?

_____

12. Jamal had 17 baseball cards. After he gave some of the cards to his brother, he had 9 cards left. How many baseball cards did Jamal give to his brother?

_____

3-1

Name _____

Homework Practice

Collect and Organize Data

Organize the set of data in a tally chart.

1. While Ryan waited for his bus, he watched cars go by and recorded the color of the cars. Here is what he saw.

   Color of cars: red, white, blue, white, tan, red, tan, blue, red, tan, blue, white, tan, red, tan, white, tan, tan, white, tan, blue, tan, blue, white, blue, tan

Color of Cars	
Color	Tally
Red	
Tan	
White	
Blue	

Organize the set of data in a frequency table.

2. Alyssa records what her friends say is their favorite day of the school week. Place this information in a frequency table.

Day	Votes
Monday	||
Tuesday	||||
Wednesday		
Thursday	||||	
Friday	|||| ||||

Day	Votes

Spiral Review

Subtract. Use addition to check.

3. 208 − 35 _____

4. $9,005 − $5,925 _____

5. 704 − 65 _____

6. 8,001 − 7,504 _____

7. 102 − 15 _____

8. $301 − $129 _____

Name _____

3-2 Homework Practice

Find Mode, Median, and Outliers

Find the mode and median of the set of data. Identify any outliers.

1. Movie ticket prices

Theaters	Plex	Multi	Cine	Matinee	Center	Theater	Main
Price	$8	$9	$10	$9	$8	$9	$10

Mode: _____   Median: _____   Outlier: _____

2. Scores in basketball games

Game	1	2	3	4	5	6	7
Score	45	57	62	59	57	55	60

Mode: _____   Median: _____   Outlier: _____

Oraganize the data in a tally chart and a frequency table. (Lesson 3-1)

3. Katherine watched students choose lunch from among four choices. Here is what she saw. Make a tally chart and frequency table of Katherine's data.

   Lunch Choices: pizza, salad, taco, pizza, sandwich, salad, taco, taco, pizza, taco, sandwich, taco, salad, pizza, taco, sandwich, salad, taco, pizza, taco, salad, pizza, sandwich, taco, pizza, taco, salad, taco, pizza

Lunch	Tally

Frequency Table:	

Grade 4   16   Chapter 3

Name _____

3-3 Homework Practice

Problem-Solving Strategy: Make a Table

Solve. Use the *make a table* strategy.

1. Rosa knits sweaters to sell. Each sweater takes 4 balls of yarn. How many balls of yarn will she need to make 23 sweaters?

   _____

2. Each ball of yarn costs $6. How much money will Rosa earn selling all 23 sweaters if she sells each sweater for $35? Remember, she has to pay for the yarn she used to make the sweaters. _____

3. Josh is a photographer. For every 7 pictures he takes, he has one portrait he can sell for $15. If Josh made $180 selling portraits, how many photographs did he take? _____

4. Hannah practices her gymnastics routine 12 times at each practice. If she practices 5 days a week, about how many times does Hannah practice her routine in 4 weeks? _____

Spiral Review

Find the mode and median of the set of data. Identify any outliers. (Lesson 3-2)

5. Students absent because of the flu

Month	Students
September	25
October	125
November	125
December	175
January	175
February	225
March	175

Mode: _____

Median: _____

Outlier: _____

6. Average travel time to school

Student	Javier	Daniel	Lourdes	Kayla	William	Amber	Kyle
Time	10	15	10	20	10	20	40

Mode: _____

Median: _____

Outlier: _____

Grade 4   Chapter 3

3-4 Homework Practice

Line Plots

Organize each set of data in a line plot.

1. Number of books checked out per person at the library.

Number of Books	People
2	8
3	6
4	6
5	6
10	1

2. Number of homeruns hit per game.

Game	Homeruns
1	4
2	4
3	0
4	1
5	3
6	4
7	2

Identify the mode, median, and any outliers for the data set.

3. Number of books checked out per person.
   Mode: _____   Median: _____   Outlier: _____

4. Number of homeruns hit per game.
   Mode: _____   Median: _____   Outlier: _____

Spiral Review   Make a table to solve. (Lesson 3-3)

5. Aaron is selling popcorn to raise money for the band. He sells 1 box of popcorn for every 3 houses he visits. How many houses will he need to visit to sell 9 boxes of popcorn? _____

6. Kimberly babysits 3 hours on weekends. For every 3 hours she works, she earns $25. If she wants to earn $165, how many weekends must she work? _____

7. If Kimberly starts working 5 hours on weekends and earns $42, how many weekends must she work to earn the $165?

Name _____

3-5 Homework Practice
Bar Graphs

For Exercises 1–4, use the graph shown.

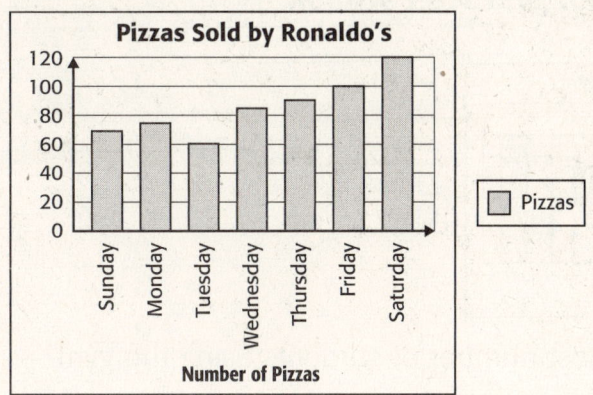

1. Which day did Ronaldo's sell the most pizzas? _____

2. How many pizzas were sold on Thursday? _____

3. What was the total number of pizzas sold on Monday and Tuesday? _____

4. How many more pizzas were sold on Saturday than Wednesday? _____

Spiral Review   (Lesson 3-4)

5. Organize the set of data in a line plot. Number of books checked out per person at the library.

Number of Books	People
4	8
6	6
7	6
8	6
19	1

6. Identify the mode, median, and any outliers for the data set. Number of books checked out per person.

Mode: _____

Median: _____

Outlier: _____

Grade 4   19   Chapter 3

Name _____

3-6

Homework Practice

Bar and Double Bar Graphs

For Exercises 1–3, use the bar graph that shows the number of students using the school gym after school.

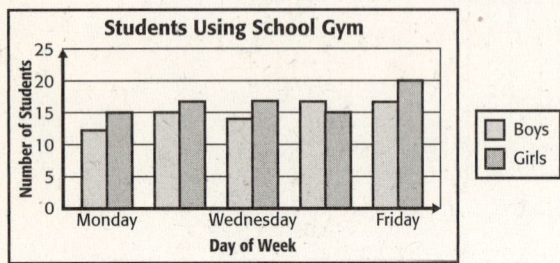

1. Which day had the most number of students using the gym?
   _____

2. Did more girls or boys use the gym after school?
   _____

3. Estimate how many boys used the gym.
   _____

Spiral Review

For Exercises 4–5, use the graph shown. (Lesson 3-5)

The graph shows the kind of books checked out by students at the library.

4. Which kind of book was most frequently checked out by students at the library? _____

5. About how many fewer art books were checked out than novels? _____

Grade 4   Chapter 3

3-7

Name _____

Homework Practice

Problem-Solving Investigation: Choose a Strategy

Use any strategy to solve. Tell what strategy you used.

1. Each night, Sabrina spends 15 minutes more doing homework than her sister Tiffany. If Tiffany spends 50 minutes in a 5-day week doing homework, how many minutes does Tiffany spend doing homework in that same week? _____

   Strategy: _____

2. Caleb is organizing his shirts. He is following a pattern: white, blue, white, red, white, blue... What color is next if this pattern continues? _____

   Strategy: _____

3. Corey has 56 people to whom he would like to send a card. If the cards come in packages of 6, how many packages does he need to buy? _____

   Strategy: _____

Spiral Review
(Lesson 3–6)

For Exercises 4-6, use the graph shown.

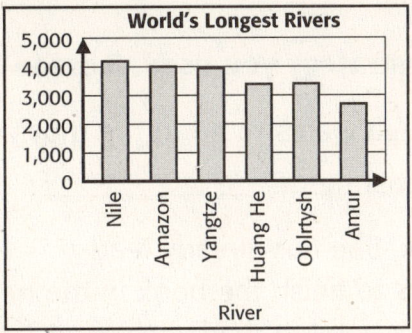

4. Which river is the longest? _____

5. About how long is the Yangtze River? _____

6. Estimate the difference in length between the Nile and the Amur Rivers. _____

Name _____

3-8 Homework Practice

Determine Possible Outcomes

Draw a tree diagram to show all the possible outcomes for each situation.

1. Choose a jacket and shoes.

Jacket	Shoes
White	Black
Black	Tan
Green	White

Spiral Review

Use any strategy to solve. Tell what strategy you used. (Lesson 3–7)

2. It costs $18 for 2 movie tickets. Thea wants to go to the movies with 3 friends. How much will it cost them? _____

3. Salma is reading a 300-page book. She has already read 60 pages of the book. If she wants to finish the book in the next 3 weeks, how many pages will she need to read each week?

   _____

4. Marcus has $15. He wants to buy as many baseball cards as he can. A pack of 10 cards costs $2.50. How many baseball cards can Marcus get? _____

Name _____

3-9 Homework Practice
Probability

Describe the probability of each outcome. Use *certain, likely, equally likely, unlikely,* or *impossible*.

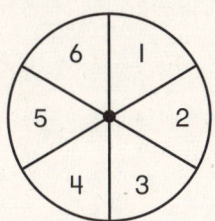

1. Spinning an even number _____
2. Spinning a 2 _____
3. Spinning a 4, 5, or 6 _____
4. Spinning a 7 _____
5. Spinning a 1, 2, 3, 4, 5, or 6 _____

Create a table to show the possible outcomes for the situation. Then, use the table to describe the probability of the outcome.

6. Jorge is picking something for dinner. He has 2 boxes of pasta, 3 boxes of rice, and 5 types of meat. If he picks one randomly, describe the probability of picking a meat.

_____

Spiral Review Draw a tree diagram to show all the possible outcomes for the situation. (Lesson 3-8)

7. Pick two cards.

4-1 Homework Practice

Relate Multiplication and Division

Write a fact family for each set of numbers.

1. 3, 6, 18

    _____   _____

    _____   _____

2. 2, 5, 10

    _____   _____

    _____   _____

3. 3 × ___ = 21   21 ÷ 7 = ___

   7 × ___ = 21   21 ÷ 3 = ___

Divide. Use a related multiplication fact.

4. 25 ÷ 5 = ___   5. 72 ÷ 9 = ___

6. 56 ÷ 8 = ___   7. 42 ÷ 7 = ___

Spiral Review

Two spinners are divided into four equal parts. The grid shows the possible outcomes when each spinner is spun once.

8. What is the probability of spinning two different colors? ___

		Second Spinner			
		Red(R)	Blue(B)	Yellow(Y)	Green(G)
First Spinner	Red (R)	RR	RB	RY	RG
	Blue (B)	BR	BB	BY	BG
	Yellow (Y)	YR	YB	YY	YG
	Green (G)	GR	GB	GY	GG

9. What is the probability of spinning a red on the first spin? ___

Grade 4 — Chapter 4

4-2

Name _____

Homework Practice

Algebra: Multiplicaton Properties and Division Rules

Identify the property shown by each number sentence.

1. $5 \times (2 \times 4) = (5 \times 2) \times 4$

   _____

2. $8 \div 8 = 1$ _____

3. $33 \times 1 = 33$

   _____

Complete each number sentence. Identify each property shown.

4. $5 \div \boxed{} = 1$ _____

5. $9 \times 8 = 8 \times \boxed{}$

   _____

6. $\boxed{} \div 12 = 0$

   _____

Spiral Review

Complete each fact family. (Lesson 4-1)

7. $6 \times 5 = \boxed{}$

   $5 \times \boxed{} = 30$

   $30 \div 5 = \boxed{}$

   $30 \div 6 = \boxed{}$

8. $7 \times 9 = \boxed{}$

   $9 \times \boxed{} = 63$

   $63 \div 7 = \boxed{}$

   $63 \div 9 = \boxed{}$

Divide. Use a related multiplication fact.

9. $20 \div 2 = $ _____

10. $49 \div 7 = $ _____

11. $72 \div 9 = $ _____

12. $56 \div 7 = $ _____

13. $42 \div 7 = $ _____

14. $32 \div 8 = $ _____

4-3

Name _____

Homework Practice

Multiply and Divide Facts Through 5

Multiply or divide.

1. 4 × 4 ____
2. 10 × 4 ____
3. 3 ÷ 1 ____
4. 2 × 6 ____
5. 2 × 3 ____
6. 12 ÷ 4 ____
7. 5 × 1 ____
8. 7 × 2 ____
9. 8 ÷ 2 ____
10. 0 × 7 ____
11. 4 × 5 ____
12. 15 ÷ 3 ____

ALGEBRA Complete each number sentence.

13. ☐ × 2 = 16
14. ☐ ÷ 5 = 4

15. 3 × 5 = ☐
16. 33 ÷ ☐ = 3

Spiral Review

Complete each number sentence. Identify the property used.
(Lesson 5-2)

17. 5 × (2 × 7) = (5 × ____) × 7

_____

18. ____ ÷ 11 = 0

_____

19. 8 × ____ = 8

_____

20. 2 × 7 = 7 × ____

_____

Grade 4   26   Chapter 4

4-4 Homework Practice

Problem-Solving Strategy: Choose an Operation

Tell which operation you would use to solve each problem. Then solve.

1. Alejandro works at a soup kitchen each week. He works for 3 hours at a time. How many hours does he work in 12 weeks?
   _____

2. There are 4 acrobats in the circus act. If they each have 5 routines, how many routines do they perform altogether?
   _____

3. Mario collects baseball cards. If he buys 4 cards a week, how many total cards will he have after 8 weeks?
   _____

4. Ann invited 4 friends over to play. They made muffins for a snack. If they made 40 muffins to divide evenly, how many will each friend have? _____

5. Rob bought the three items below. If he paid with three $10 bills, how much change will he get back? _____

Item	Cost
Swimsuit	$12
Goggles	$5
Towel	$8

 **Multiply or divide.** (Lesson 4-3)

6. 6 × 4 = _____   7. 8 × 5 = _____   8. 7 × 5 = _____

9. 15 ÷ 5 = _____   10. 18 ÷ 3 = _____   11. 3 × 4 = _____

12. 7 × 6 = _____   13. 8 × 4 = _____   14. 8 × 7 = _____

Grade 4 — Chapter 4

4-5

Name _____

Reteach

Multiply and Divide Facts Through 10

Multiply

Find 4 × 5.
Think: Skip count by 5s four times.

You can skip count with nickels to multiply by 5.

5   10   15   20

4 × 5 = 20

Divide

Find 30 ÷ 6.
Think: How many groups of 6 are in 30?

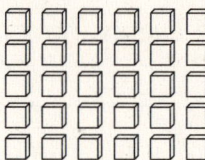

6 × ? = 30 → 5 × 6 = 30
There are 5 groups of 6 in 30. So, 30 ÷ 6 = 5.

Multiply or divide.

1. 7 × 5 = ____
2. 21 ÷ 3 = ____
3. 10)30 ____

4. 8 × 6 = ____
5. 20 ÷ 5 = ____
6. 11)33 ____

7. 9 × 8 = ____
8. 12 ÷ 2 = ____
9. 12)36 ____

10.   5
    × 8

11.   10
    × 9

12.   6
    × 6

Name _____

4-6

Homework Practice

Multiply with 11 and 12

1. 11 × 6 ____
2. 12 ÷ 3 ____
3. 5)55 ____

4. 3 × 12 ____
5. 44 ÷ 4 ____
6. 12)60 ____

7. 5 × 11 ____
8. 99 ÷ 9 ____
9. 11)88 ____

10. 12 × 8 ____
11. 96 ÷ 12 ____
12. 5)65 ____

13. 11
    × 5

14. 11
    × 3

15. 12
    × 6

16. 11
    × 2

17. 12
    × 2

18. 12
    × 9

19.   7
    × 11

20.   7
    × 12

ALGEBRA Solve.

21. Nia has 96 people invited to her family reunion. Each table can hold 12 people. How many tables will be needed?

_____

22. Nia is painting a fence. She is painting 12 boards an hour. How many hours will it take her to paint 108 boards? _____

Spiral Review

Multiply or divide. (Lesson 4-5)

23. 12 ÷ 6 = ___
24. 7 × 2 = ____
25. 18 ÷ 3 = ___

26. 4 × 5 = ____
27. 30 ÷ 6 = ___
28. 6 × 4 = ____

Grade 4

4-7

Name _____

Homework Practice

Problem-Solving Investigation: Choose a Strategy

Use the make a table strategy or choose an operation to solve each problem.

1. Jayden has read 22 pages of the newspaper. Adrian has read 42 pages. How many pages have they read altogether?

   _____

2. Sergio was building a model plane. It took 6 days to build the model. If he worked for 4 hours a day, how many total hours did he take to complete the model? What if it took 7 days? 8 days?

   _____

3. If there are 24 pieces of popcorn in a serving, and you eat 72 pieces, how many total servings have you consumed?

   _____

4. How many pieces of popcorn will you need for 4 people allowing 1 serving per person?

   _____

5. Catalina, Jose, and Diego went to get a pizza. If they spent $18 altogether and they split the bill evenly, what did they each pay?

   _____

Spiral Review

Multiply or divide. (Lesson 4-6)

6. $24 \div 12 =$ _____

7. $12 \div 3 =$ _____

8. $4 \times 3 =$ _____

9. $33 \div 3 =$ _____

10. $7 \times 11 =$ _____

11. $12 \times 6 =$ _____

12. A school bus can fit 4 passengers in each row. If you have a bus with 12 rows, how many students can fit on it? _____

13. Look back over this page. Circle all the answers on this page that are less than 20.

Grade 4   Chapter 4

4-8 Homework Practice

Algebra: Multiply Three Numbers

Multiply.

1. 5 × 2 × 7 = ____
2. 8 × 3 × 2 = ____
3. 4 × 2 × 5 = ____
4. 5 × 4 × 4 = ____
5. 8 × 3 × 2 = ____
6. 4 × 2 × 5 = ____
7. 7 × 2 × 6 = ____
8. 9 × 4 × 2 = ____
9. 10 × 12 × 1 = ____
10. 7 × 2 × 6 = ____
11. 9 × 4 × 2 = ____
12. 0 × 12 × 1 = ____

ALGEBRA Copy and complete each number sentence.

13. 4 × ☐ × 8 = 64 ____
14. 6 × 4 × ☐ = 240 ____
15. 4 × ☐ × 8 = 64 ____
16. 6 × 4 × ☐ = 240 ____
17. 5 × 3 × 4 = ☐ ____
18. 10 × 11 × ☐ = 770 ____
19. 5 × 3 × 4 = ☐ ____
20. 10 × 11 × ☐ = 770 ____

21. If you walk 3 miles a day 3 days a week, how many miles will you walk in 9 weeks? ____

Spiral Review

Use the make a table strategy or choose an operation to solve each problem. (Lesson 4-7)

22. A boat can fit 2 passengers in each row. How many people can fit in a boat with 8 rows? ____

23. If you and 3 friends go to a movie and pay $36 for your tickets, how much do you each pay? ____

24. Carleen has 36 roses to put into 3 vases. How many roses should go into each vase if she wants each vase to have an equal number? ____

Name _____

4-9 Homework Practice

Factors and Multiples

Find all of the factors of each number.

1. 2 _____
2. 4 _____
3. 14 _____
4. 20 _____
5. 33 _____
6. 37 _____

Identify the first five multiples for each number.

7. 2 ___, ___, ___, ___, ___

8. 3 ___, ___, ___, ___, ___

9. 6 ___, ___, ___, ___, ___

10. 8 ___, ___, ___, ___, ___

11.  If you eat 1 banana each day, how many bananas will you eat in 12 days? In 10, 11, and 13 days? ____, ____, ____, ____

Spiral Review

Multiply. (Lesson 4–8)

12. $4 \times 1 \times 3$ _____

13. $5 \times 2 \times 4$ _____

14. $3 \times 2 \times 12$ _____

15. $5 \times 1 \times 12$ _____

16. $11 \times 2 \times 3$ _____

17. $4 \times 6 \times 10$ _____

5-1 Homework Practice
Addition and Subtraction Expressions

Find the value of each expression if $y = 7$ and $b = 2$.

1. $y + 6$ _____
2. $14 - b$ _____
3. $(y - 1) + 3$ _____
4. $b + 8$ _____
5. $y + 18$ _____
6. $19 - (b + 3)$ _____
7. $y - 2$ _____
8. $12 + b$ _____
9. $y + (14 - 9)$ _____

Write an expression for each situation.

10. four more than j ___+___
11. v minus fifteen ___−___
12. the sum of k and twelve ___+___
13. twenty-three subtracted from x ___−___

Write an expression for each situation. Then find the value of the expression to answer the question.

14. John walks 5 minutes longer to school than Rosa. If Rosa walks 24 minutes to school, how long does John walk to school?
    ___+___

15. Caroline is 7 inches shorter than Kevin. Kevin is 56 inches tall. How tall is Caroline?
    ___−___

Spiral Review

Find all of the factors of each number.

16. $5 =$ _____
17. $3 =$ _____
18. $12 =$ _____
19. $22 =$ _____
20. $7 =$ _____
21. $14 =$ _____
22. $6 =$ _____
23. $10 =$ _____
24. $25 =$ _____
25. $35 =$ _____

5-2 Homework Practice

Name _____

Solve Equations Mentally

Solve each equation mentally.

1. $3 + d = 11$ _____
2. $15 - r = 2$ _____
3. $f + 4 = 10$ _____
4. $20 = t + 7$ _____
5. $13 - h = 4$ _____
6. $9 = w - 12$ _____
7. $j - 2 = 19$ _____
8. $12 = 3 + z$ _____
9. $6 + m = 17$ _____
10. $17 - b = 4$ _____

Write and solve an equation for each situation.

11. A number plus 5 equals 13. What is the number?
    _____

12. Twelve less than a number equals 25. What is the number?
    _____

13. The sum of 4 and a number is 27. What is the number?
    _____

14. Seven subtracted from a number is 15. What is the number?
    _____

Spiral Review

Find the value of each expression if $x = 6$ and $c = 4$. (Lesson 5-1)

15. $x + 3$ _____
16. $10 + c$ _____
17. $c + 12$ _____
18. $(x - 2) + 7$ _____
19. $x - 5$ _____
20. $22 - (c + 3)$ _____

Write an expression for each situation.

21. seven more than d _____
22. w minus 12 _____
23. the sum of f and seventeen _____
24. twenty-one subtracted from p _____

Name _____

5-3 Homework Practice

Problem-Solving Skill: Extra and Missing Information

Identify any missing or extra information. Then solve if possible.

1. At the kennel, the staff walks each dog 2 times per day. They walk 3 dogs at a time. How many dogs do they take for a walk each day?

   _____

   _____

2. Each week, Michelle will invite 1 girl from her class to come home with her. There are 17 boys in her class and 15 other girls. How many weeks will it take to invite every girl to come home with her?

   _____

   _____

3. Patrick loves vegetables. Every day for school he packs a small bag of carrots, a small bag of celery, and a small bag of broccoli. He also likes apple juice. How many small bags of vegetables does Patrick bring to school in a week?

   _____

   _____

4. Nicole wants to buy a turkey sandwich, chips, and a bottle of water for lunch. She has $5 with her. Does she have enough?

   _____

   _____

Spiral Review

Solve each equation mentally. (Lesson 5-2)

5. $5 + d = 9$ _____

6. $22 - r = 7$ _____

7. $f + 7 = 20$ _____

8. $24 = t + 6$ _____

9. $16 - h = 5$ _____

10. $12 = w - 11$ _____

11. $j - 7 = 12$ _____

12. $9 = 4 + z$ _____

13. $5 + m = 14$ _____

14. $18 = 11 + t$ _____

5-4 Homework Practice

Identify, Describe, and Extend Patterns

Find the rule for each pattern.

1. 39, 40, 36, 37, 33, 34 _____
2. 29, 42, 55, 68, 81, 94 _____
3. 64, 55, 46, 37, 28, 19 _____
4. 12, 7, 14, 9, 16, 11 _____
5. 19, 25, 31, 37, 43, 49 _____
6. 53, 49, 52, 48, 51, 54 _____
7. 71, 73, 68, 70, 65, 67 _____
8. 48, 42, 36, 30, 24, 18 _____

Find the next number in each pattern.

9. 67, 81, 95, 109, 123, ☐
10. 55, 52, 49, 46, 43, ☐
11. 22, 27, 26, 31, 30, ☐
12. 83, 94, 105, 116, 127, ☐
13. 9, 11, 13, 15, 17, ☐
14. 35, 30, 25, 20, 15, ☐
15. 48, 40, 32, 24, 16, ☐
16. 24, 36, 35, 47, 46, ☐

Spiral Review
Identify any missing or extra information. Then solve if possible. (Lesson 5-3)

17. Brigit, Parker, and Spencer want to go to a play. What is the total cost of their tickets?

_____

_____

18. The bake sale is selling 4 mini muffins for $1. How many muffins can Andrea buy?

_____

_____

5-5 Homework Practice

Function Tables: Find a Rule (+, −)

Complete the input/output table for each equation.

1.
Rule: $e + 7 = f$	
Input (e)	Output (f)

2.
Rule: $g - 4 = h$	
Input (g)	Output (h)

Input (s)	Output (f)
2	$27
4	$29
6	
8	
10	

3. A dance studio offers lessons to students. It costs $25 to rent the studio plus $1 per student. Use the table to write an equation for this situation. _____

4. Find how much it will cost if 6, 8, and 10 students take lessons.

_____

Spiral Review

Create an input/output table for each equation. (Lesson 5-4)

5. $e + 5 = f$

Rule: $e + 5 = f$	
Input (e)	Output (f)

6. $g - 8 = h$

Rule: $g - 8 = h$	
Input (g)	Output (h)

5-6 Homework Practice

Multiplication and Division Expressions

Find the value of each expression if $j = 12$ and $k = 6$.

1. $j \div 3$ _____
2. $k \div 2$ _____
3. $3 \times j$ _____
4. $5 \times k$ _____
5. $j \times k$ _____
6. $j \div k$ _____
7. $5 \times (j \div 4)$ _____
8. $(18 \div k) \div 3$ _____
9. $(j \div k) \times 5$ _____

Write an expression for each situation.

10. a number multiplied by 3 _____

11. the product of 5 and a number _____

12. 16 divided by a number _____

13. a number divided by 8 _____

14. Three times a week, Savannah does yard work for her neighbors for 2 hours. If she is paid $5 per hour, how much does she earn each week? Write an expression using *m* for money and solve.

_____

Spiral Review

Find the value of each expression if $q = 15$ and $r = 5$. (Lesson 5-5)

15. $q \div 5$ _____

16. $4 \times r$ _____

17. $5 \times (q \div 5)$ _____

18. $(20 \div r) \div 2$ _____

Write an expression for each situation.

19. 6 multiplied by a number _____

20. a number divided by 5 _____

21. Each of three friends can decorate 3 pencil boxes a day. Write an expression to show how many pencil boxes the friends can decorate in *d* days.

_____

Grade 4 — Chapter 5

5-7 Homework Practice

Problem-Solving Investigation: Choose a Strategy

Use any strategy shown below to solve. Tell which strategy you used.

- Draw a picture
- Look for a pattern
- Make a table

1. Allison can read 4 pages of her book in 8 minutes. How many minutes will it take her to read 16 pages of her book?

   _____

   Strategy: _____

2. Richard can clean his room in 22 minutes. Corey can clean his room in 25 minutes, and Brooke can clean her room in 21 minutes. If they have to clean their rooms twice a week, how many minutes do all three spend cleaning their rooms each week?

   _____

   Strategy: _____

3. Complete the number pattern.

   45, 43, 42, 40, 39, ____, ____, ____, ____

   Strategy: _____

Spiral Review

Find the value of each expression if $g = 14$ and $h = 7$. (Lesson 5-6)

4. $g \div 2$ _____
5. $h \times 7$ _____
6. $g \div h$ _____
7. $6h$ _____
8. $(g \div 2) \times 8$ _____
9. $4 \times (h \div 1)$ _____
10. $g \times h$ _____
11. $(g \div h) \times 12$ _____
12. $3 \times h$ _____

5-8 Homework Practice

Function Tables: Find a Rule (×, ÷)

Write an equation that describes the pattern. Then use the equation to find the next three numbers.

1. Rule: _____

Input (v)	Output (w)
8	4
12	6
16	
20	
24	

2. Rule: _____

Input (x)	Output (y)
5	15
10	30
15	
20	
25	

3. Shannon found out there are four yellow pencils for every one blue pencil. Make a table to find how many yellow pencils there would be if she found 5, 7, 9, 11, and 13 blue pencils.

Rule: _____	
Blue Pencils Input (x)	Yellow Pencils Output (y)

Spiral Review

Use any strategy to solve. Tell what strategy you used. (Lesson 5-7)

4. In Alexa's neighborhood, there are 3 times as many dogs as birds. There are 5 more cats than birds. There are 24 cats. How many dogs are there? _____ Strategy: _____

Grade 4 — Chapter 5

Name _____

8-1 Homework Practice

Division with Remainders

Divide. Check each answer.

1. 6)56 _____
2. 5)42 _____
3. 6)25 _____

4. 2)32 _____
5. 5)41 _____
6. 9)53 _____

7. 6)54 _____
8. 6)34 _____
9. 8)21 _____

10. 7)35 _____
11. 72 ÷ 8 _____
12. 15 ÷ 7 _____

13. 64 ÷ 7 _____
14. 49 ÷ 3 _____
15. 28 ÷ 3 _____

16. Andy's mom would not tell her age, but she did give these clues:

    Divide my age by 4, and it is 10. I am between 50 and 30. _____

 (Lesson 7-7)

Multiply.

17. 63 × 99 _____

18. 144 × 33 _____

19. 706 × 67 _____

20. 4,371 × 42 _____

21. Through his telescope, Jose identified 12 stars each night for 64 nights. How many different stars has Jose seen? _____

22. Look back over this page. Circle all of the numbers on the page that can be divided by 2 without a remainder.

_____

8-2

Name _____

Homework Practice

Divide Multiples of 10, 100, and 1,000

Divide. Use patterns.

1. 6)300 _____
2. 5)2,000 _____
3. 4)3,600 _____
4. 2)1,000 _____
5. 6)1,200 _____
6. 5)1,000 _____
7. 2)1,800 _____
8. 8)4,000 _____
9. 9)2,700 _____
10. 8)3,200 _____
11. 4)4,000 _____
12. 3)2,100 _____
13. 5)3,500 _____
14. 6)2,400 _____
15. 7)2,800 _____

Complete the table.

16. Divide by 5.

Input	Output
1,500	_____
3,000	_____
6,000	_____

Spiral Review

Divide. Check each answer. (Lesson 8-1)

17. 61 ÷ 3 _____
18. 21 ÷ 5 _____
19. 80 ÷ 7 _____
20. 12 ÷ 5 _____
21. 14 ÷ 6 _____
22. 51 ÷ 7 _____
23. 28 ÷ 6 _____
24. 72 ÷ 3 _____

25. Mrs. Jones has 36 calculators. She has to divide them between 3 groups of students. How many calculators will each group get?

_____

Name _____

8-3 Homework Practice

Problem-Solving Strategy: Guess and Check

Solve. Use the guess and check strategy.

1. Jim's baseball team has played 5 games so far this season. Jim hit 5 home runs. Justin hit twice as many home runs as Jim hit. They are the only boys who have hit home runs this season. How many home runs have been hit? _____

2. Joe's parents have used 29 gallons of gasoline this month. Last month, June, they used twice that amount. The month before, May, they used twice what they did in June. How many gallons of gasoline did they use in May? _____

3. 510 is the total number of tickets that can be sold for the baseball game. If the school bought 25 tickets and a neighborhood club bought twice as many tickets as the school, how many tickets can still be sold? _____

4. Linda bought three items from the list below.

   peanuts $1, a ring $5, a coloring book $3, a stuffed animal $6

   She gave the cashier $10 and got no change. Which three items did she buy?

   _____
   _____

Spiral Review

Divide. Use patterns. (Lesson 8-2)

5. 2)200 _____

6. 8)400 _____

7. 3)1,500 _____

8. 2,400 ÷ 6 _____

9. 3,600 ÷ 6 _____

10. 5,600 ÷ 7 _____

8-4 Homework Practice

Estimate Quotients

Estimate. Check your estimate.

1. 8)242 _____
2. 8)641 _____
3. 5)402 _____
4. 6)241 _____
5. 7)563 _____
6. 4)121 _____
7. 3)273 _____
8. 5)149 _____
9. 8)161 _____
10. 7)494 _____
11. 9)184 _____
12. 9)629 _____
13. 3)301 _____
14. 9)453 _____
15. 6)331 _____
16. 2)804 _____
17. 6)422 _____
18. 5)247 _____
19. 9)625 _____
20. 8)639 _____

Spiral Review

Solve. Use the guess and check strategy. (Lesson 9-3)

21. Phil had 3 baseball cards. One of them cost twice as much as the other two. If the total amount that he paid for the cards was $40, how much did each card cost? _____

22. Jan's mother said that Jan could have 2 tickets to a movie, 5 tickets for fruit smoothies, or 7 tickets for rides at an amusement park. Jan had to choose what she wanted. Each ticket was worth $5. Jan's mother spent a total of $10. What did Jan choose?

_____

23. Look back over this page and circle all the numbers that can be rounded to 300. Then draw a box around any numbers that can be rounded to 600. _____

Name _____

8-5 Homework Practice

Two-Digit Quotients

Divide. Use estimation to check.

1. 21 ÷ 4 _____
2. 89 ÷ 6 _____
3. 170 ÷ 3 _____
4. 442 ÷ 5 _____
5. 712 ÷ 8 _____
6. 145 ÷ 3 _____
7. 165 ÷ 9 _____
8. 368 ÷ 7 _____
9. 125 ÷ 7 _____
10. 219 ÷ 4 _____
11. 324 ÷ 9 _____
12. 364 ÷ 7 _____
13. 498 ÷ 5 _____
14. 642 ÷ 7 _____
15. 432 ÷ 8 _____
16. 681 ÷ 7 _____
17. 251 ÷ 8 _____
18. 219 ÷ 7 _____
19. 868 ÷ 9 _____
20. 765 ÷ 8 _____

 **Estimate. Check your estimate.** (Lesson 8-4)

21. 254 ÷ 5 _____

22. 349 ÷ 7 _____

23. 639 ÷ 8 _____

24. 487 ÷ 7 _____

25. Look back over the page. Circle all numbers that can be divided in half with no remainder. _____

8-6

Name _____

Homework Practice

Problem-Solving Investigation: Choose a Strategy

Use any strategy to solve.

- Use for a pattern
- Work backward
- Guess and check
- Make a table
- Act it out

1. Ellie has 22 coins that equal $3.85. What are the coins?

   _____

2. Meg is going to a birthday party at 6 p.m. She gets home from school at 3 p.m. It will take her 1 hour to do her homework, 30 minutes to get dressed, and 30 minutes to get to the party. How much extra time does she have?

   _____

3. Sandy is creating a flower basket with 12 white, yellow, and orange flowers in it. The order she wants the flowers is white, orange, yellow. If she always has a white beside an orange and a yellow beside an orange, how many orange flowers will she need to have?

   _____

4. What is the next number in the pattern 20,000; 4,000; 800; 160; ____

   What is the pattern?

   _____

Spiral Review

Divide. Use estimation to check. (Lesson 8–5)

5. $2\overline{)57}$ _____

6. $4\overline{)79}$ _____

7. $5\overline{)86}$ _____

8. $2\overline{)93}$ _____

9. $3\overline{)46}$ _____

10. $8\overline{)99}$ _____

8-7

Name _____

Homework Practice

Three-Digit Quotients

Divide. Use estimation to check.

1. 5)569

2. 2)873

3. 5)675

4. 4)845

5. 3)334

6. 6)727

7. 8)895

8. 5)567

9. 9)999

10. 4)850

11. 3)673

12. 7)849

13. 5)997

14. 8)978

15. 7)987

16. 3)673

17. 6)674

18. 5)584

19. 3)534

20. 5)563

Spiral Review Use any strategy to solve. (Lesson 8-6)

21. What is the next number in the pattern 16, 32, 64, 128, ___ ?
    What is the pattern?

    _____

22. Janice has 8 coins that total 80 cents. What are the coins?

    _____

8-8 Homework Practice

Quotients with Zeros

Divide. Use estimation to check.

1. 5)512
2. 3)624
3. 4)837
4. 7)764
5. 3)926
6. 9)943
7. 2)642
8. 4)813
9. 4)436
10. 2)218
11. 5)543
12. 6)643
13. 3)629
14. 4)839
15. 6)658
16. 6)643
17. 4)822
18. 3)319
19. 2)611
20. 9)984

Spiral Review

Divide. Use estimation to check. (Lesson 8-7)

21. 7)878
22. 3)561
23. 6)684
24. 8)937

Solve.

25. 4 plums fit in a box. How many boxes can be filled with 968 plums?

Name _____

8-9 Homework Practice

Divide Greater Numbers

Divide. Use estimation to check.

1. 5)5,098 2. 6)6,485

3. 2)$3,458 4. 6)7,349

5. 7)8,655 6. 5)5,437

7. 9)$9,950 8. 8)8,349

9. 3)6,980 10. 2)8,642

11. 3)$4,743 12. 5)$8,115

13. 3)8,765 14. 2)6,567

15. 4)8,219 16. 3)9,651

17. 4)8,633 18. 4)3,683

Spiral Review

Divide. Use estimation to check. (Lesson 9-8)

19. 4)427 20. 6)641

21. 2)815 22. 3)929

23. 7)745 24. 3)629

25. Look back over the page. Circle all the numbers that can be rounded to a number greater than 9,000. _____

Grade 4 63 Chapter 8

Name _____

9-1 Homework Practice

Three-Dimensional Figures

Tell the number of faces, edges and vertices. Then identify each figure.

1.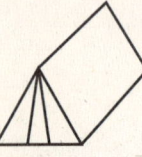

   _____
   _____
   _____

2.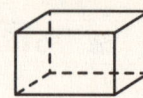

   _____
   _____
   _____

Identify the three-dimensional figure each net makes.

3.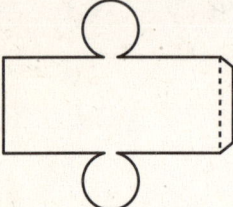

   _____

4.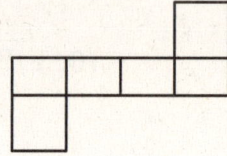

   _____

5. This three-dimensional figure has 0 faces, 0 edges, and 0 vertices. What is it?

   _____

Spiral Review   Divide. Use estimation to check. (Lesson 8-9)

6.

   _____

7. $5{,}250 \div 5 =$

   _____

8. Raul pays $43 total for lunch each month. About how much does he pay in a week?

   _____

Grade 4   64   Chapter 9

Name _____

9-2 Homework Practice

Two-Dimensional Figures

Identify each polygon.

1. 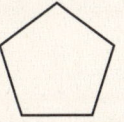 _____

2. 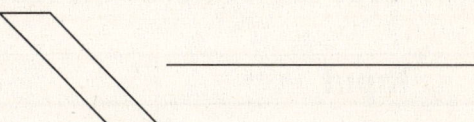 _____

3. 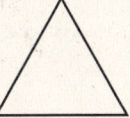 _____

4. 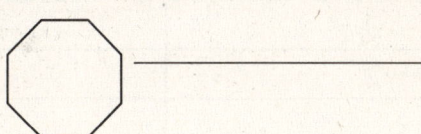 _____

Identify the shapes in the figure.

5. 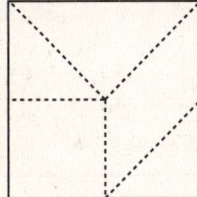 _____

Tell whether the shape is a polygon.

6. 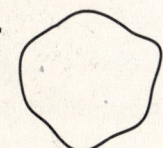 _____

7. 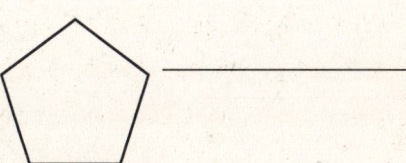 _____

Spiral Review   Identify each figure. Then tell how many faces, edges and vertices it has. (Lesson 9-1)

8.

_____

_____

9.

_____

_____

Identify the solid figure each net makes.

10.  _____

Grade 4   65   Chapter 9

9-3

Name _____

Homework Practice

Problem-Solving Strategy: Look for a Pattern

1. **ALGEBRA** Copy and complete the table. What is the pattern?

Input	Output
4	16
9	36
2	8
	24
3	

Pattern? _____

2. Describe the pattern below. Then find the missing number.

   1, 3, 9, _____ , 81

Spiral Review
Identify each polygon. (Lesson 9-2)

3.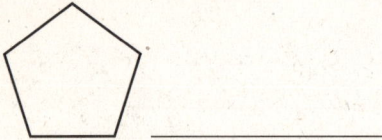

4.

5.

6.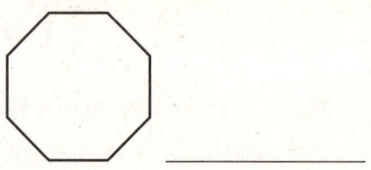

Identify the shapes in the figure.

7.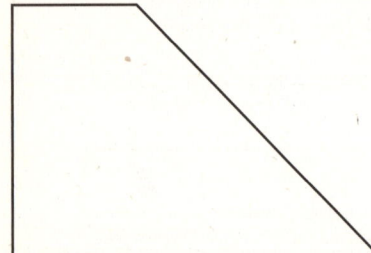

Tell whether the shape is a polygon.

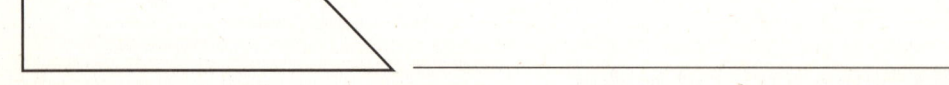

8.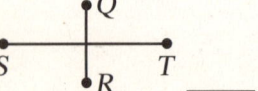

9.

10.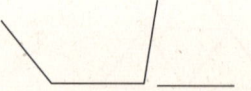

Grade 4 — 66 — Chapter 9

9-4 Homework Practice

Angles

Write the measure of the angle in degrees and as a fraction of a full turn.

1.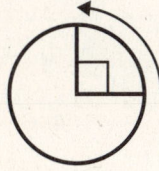

2.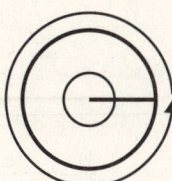

_____   _____

Classify each angle as *right*, *acute*, or *obtuse*.

3.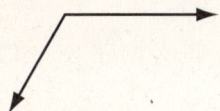

4.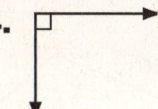

5.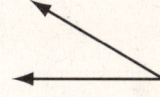

_____   _____   _____

Spiral Review

Solve. (Lesson 9-3)

6. Starting at 6:15 A.M., the subway Melissa takes leaves every 15 minutes. If she arrives at the station at 8:07 A.M., what time will the next subway train arrive?

   _____

7. Describe the pattern below. Then find the missing number.

   1, 4, 16, ____, 256   Pattern _____.

8. Complete the table. What is the pattern?

Input	Output
8	72
3	27
	63
6	

_____.

Grade 4 — Chapter 9

Name _____

9-5

Homework Practice

Triangles

Classify each triangle. Use *acute*, *right*, or *obtuse* and *equilateral*, *isosceles*, or *scalene*.

1.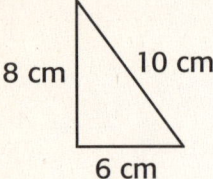

2.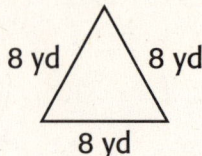

_____
_____

3.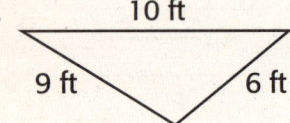

4.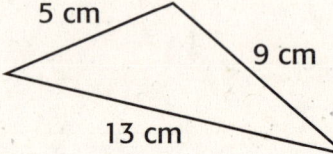

_____
_____

Spiral Review Write the measure of the angle in degrees and as a fraction of a full turn. (Lesson 9-4)

5.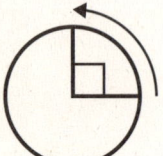

_____

6.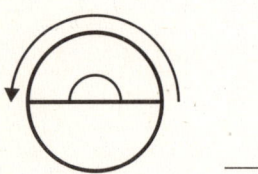

_____

Classify each angle as *right*, *acute*, or *obtuse*.

7.

8.

Name _____

9-6 Homework Practice

Quadrilaterals

Write the type of quadrilateral that best describes the shape.

1.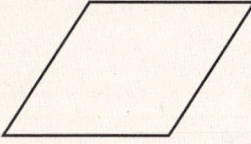

2.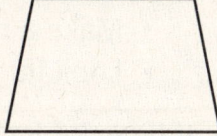

3.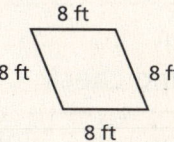

4.

5.

6.

Spiral Review Classify each triangle. Use *isosceles*, *equilateral*, or *scalene* and *acute*, *right*, or *obtuse*. (Lesson 9–5)

7.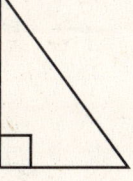

8.

9.

10.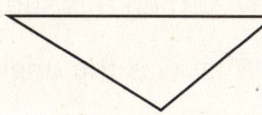

11.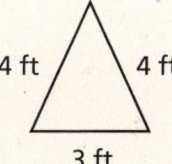

12.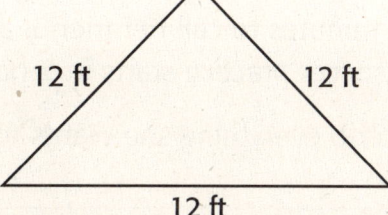

9-7

Name _____

Homework Practice

Problem-Solving Investigation: Choose a Strategy

Use any method shown below to solve. Tell what method you used.

- Act it out
- Guess and check
- Make a table
- Look for a pattern

1. Justin can run 2 blocks in 1 minute. If he is 8 blocks from home, can he can run home in 5 minutes?

   _____

   Strategy: _____

2. Sarah watched the band march by in a pattern. She saw a trumpet, flute, saxophone, drum, trumpet, flute, saxophone, drum pattern. What are the next three instruments she will see?

   _____

   Strategy: _____

Use any strategy shown below to solve. (Lesson 9-6)
Tell what strategy you used.

- Work backward
- Act it out
- Guess and check
- Look for a pattern

3. A number is multiplied by 3. Then 8 is subtracted from the product. The result is 4. What was the original number? _____

   Strategy: _____

4. Rebecca wants to bake banana bread, do her homework, call her friend, and clean her room before soccer practice. It takes 65 minutes to make banana bread, 35 minutes to do her homework, 20 minutes to call her friend, and 15 minutes to clean her room. Her soccer practice starts in 2 hours. Does she have enough time to do everything she wants to do? _____

   Strategy: _____

10-1

Name _____ Date _____

Homework Practice

Locate Points on a Number Line

Name each point represented by a letter.

1.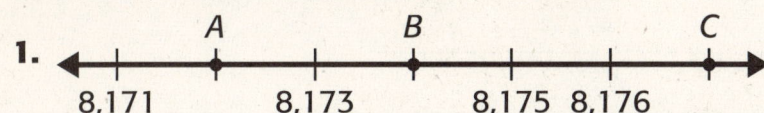
   8,171   8,173   8,175 8,176

   A = _____   B = _____   C = _____

2.
   45,902 45,904   45,908

   D = _____   E = _____   F = _____

Name the point P represents on each number line.

3.
   275,000   300,000   325,000

   P = _____

4.
   17,600   17,800   18,000   18,200

   P = _____

Spiral Review

Solve. (Lesson 9-7)

5. Identify seven bills with the total worth $20 using $1, $5, $10, and $20 bills.

   _____

6. A number is multiplied by three. Then 5 is subtracted from the product. The result is 22. What was the original number? _____

7. Jennifer has $18. She earns $6 a week for doing chores. Is it reasonable to say that Jennifer will be able to buy a new DVD player that costs $70 in 10 weeks? Explain.

   _____

   _____

10-2 Homework Practice

Lines, Line Segments, and Rays

Identify each figure.

1. _____

2. _____

3. _____

Describe the figure.

4. _____

5. _____

6. _____

Draw an example of each.

7. ray CD

8. line segment FG

Spiral Review

Write the number represented by each letter. (Lesson 10-1)

9.

A = _____   B = _____   C = _____

10.

R = _____   S = _____   T = _____

Name _____ Date _____

10-3 Homework Practice

Problem-Solving Strategy: Make an Organized List

Solve. Use the make an organized list strategy.

1. Koko has red shorts and blue shorts, and a print shirt, a T-shirt, or a tank top to wear. How many different outfits can he choose from?

   _____

2. Parker is handing out snacks. He has a large bag that is filled with smaller snack-sized bags. There is one bag of each of the following: peanuts, almonds, walnuts, mixed nuts, macadamia nuts, and cashews. What is the probability of picking a bag of macadamia nuts or almonds? How about cashews, almonds, or peanuts?

   _____

3. Martin's older brother wanted to buy a leather bomber jacket. It cost $190. He makes $38 each weekend mowing lawns and weeding gardens for neighbors. How many weekends will he need to work in order to buy the jacket?

   _____

4. Your teacher has 3 different stickers she can choose from including smiley faces, animals, or hearts. What is the probability of her choosing a heart if she picks one without looking?

   _____

Spiral Review   Describe the figure. (Lesson 10-2)

5.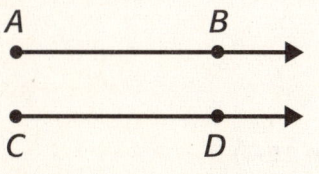

6.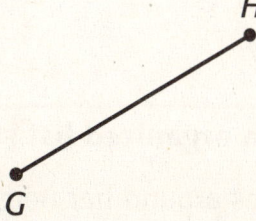

_____   _____

Grade 4   73   Chapter 10

Name _____ Date _____

10-4 Homework Practice

Find Points on a Grid

Write the ordered pair that names each point.

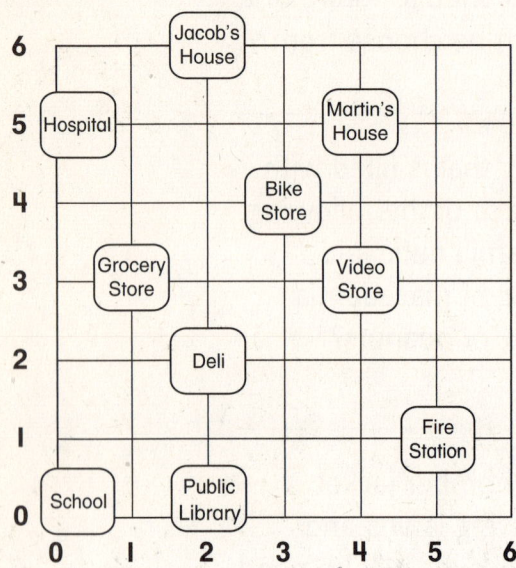

1. Deli _____
2. Bike store _____
3. Hospital _____
4. Fire Station _____

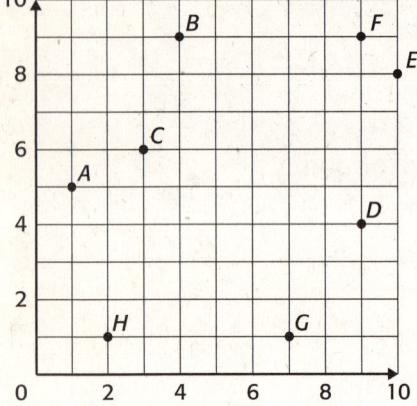

5. C _____
6. E _____
7. B _____
8. H _____

Spiral Review

Solve. Use the make an organized list strategy. (Lesson 10-3)

9. Madeline bikes 4 laps around her neighborhood 2 times a week. How many laps does she bike in 8 weeks?

_____

Grade 4   74   Chapter 10

10-5 Homework Practice

Rotations, Reflections, and Translations

Identify each transformation. Write rotation, reflection, or translation.

1.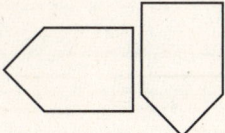

2.

3.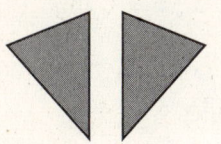

4.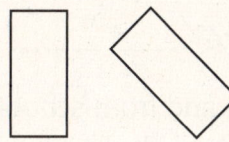

5.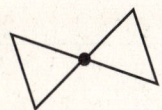

6.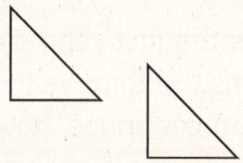

Spiral Review

Identify the building that is located at each ordered pair. (Lesson 10-4)

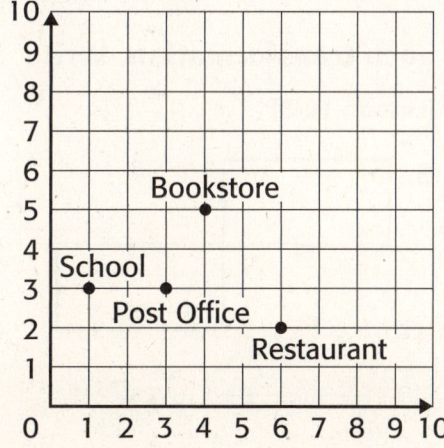

7. (4, 5) _____

8. (1, 3) _____

9. (6, 2) _____

10. (3, 3) _____

10-6 Homework Practice

Problem-Solving Investigation: Choose a Strategy

Solve using any strategy shown below.

- Use logical reasoning
- Make a model
- Draw a picture
- Work backward
- Make an organized list

1. Sydney is a receptionist and needs to make 28 phone calls. If she can make 4 phone calls in an hour, will she be able to make all of her calls in an 8 hour day? If so, how many additional phone calls will she be able to make? _____

2. Wanda rides her bike to and from school every day. She rides $\frac{3}{4}$ mile one way. How many miles will she bike in 1 week? 2 weeks?

_____

3. Nora made 4 photo albums the first year, 4 photo albums the second year, 3 photo albums the third year, and 3 photo albums the fourth year. If the pattern continues, how many photo albums will she make the fifth and sixth years? _____

4. Lola can choose from a blue sweatshirt, brown sweatshirt, or green sweatshirt, with brown boots, black boots, or tennis shoes. How many combinations can she wear? _____

Spiral Review Identify each transformation. Write rotation, reflection, or translation. (Lesson 10-5)

5.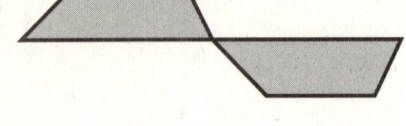
_____

6.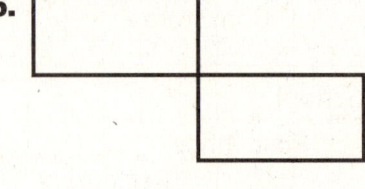
_____

Name _____ Date _____

10-7 Homework Practice

Congruent Figures

Tell whether the figures appear to be congruent. Write *yes* or *no*.

1. 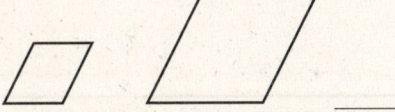 _____

2. 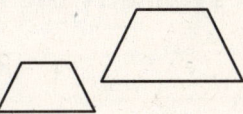 _____

3. 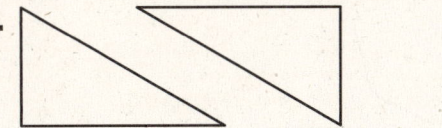 _____

4. 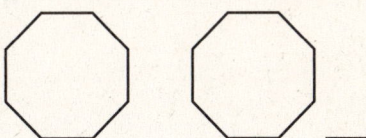 _____

5. 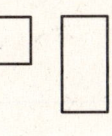 _____

6. 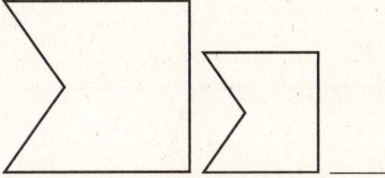 _____

Spiral Review   Solve using any strategy. (Lesson 10-6)

7. Taylor is planting 4 trees at the community center. She wants to leave a 2 square foot area between each one. How many square feet does she need for the trees?

   _____

8. Libby walks to and from her grandmother's house every day. She walks $\frac{1}{2}$ mile one way. How many miles will she walk in 2 weeks?

   _____

9. Garrett made 12 cupcakes. He sold 8 of them for 10¢ each. Then he baked 6 more cupcakes and sold them all. How many cupcakes did Garrett make in all?

10-8

Name _____ Date _____

Homework Practice

Symmetry

Tell whether each figure has line symmetry. Write *yes* or *no*. Then tell how many lines of symmetry the figure has.

1.  _____

2. 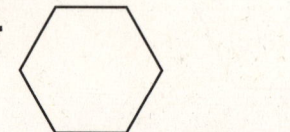 _____

3.  _____

4. 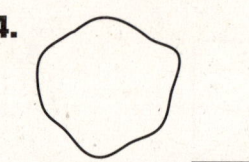 _____

Tell whether the dotted line is a line of symmetry. Write *yes* or *no*.

5. 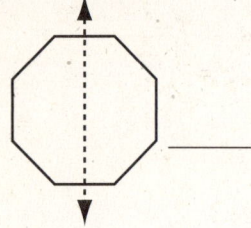 _____

6. 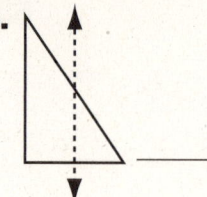 _____

7. 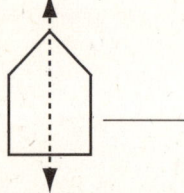 _____

8. 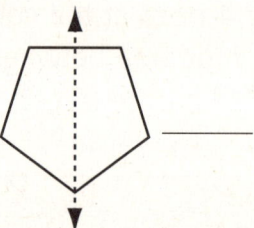 _____

Spiral Review   Tell whether the figures are congruent. Write *yes* or *no*. (Lesson 10-7)

9. 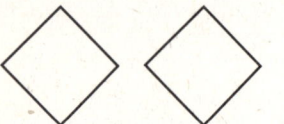 _____

10. 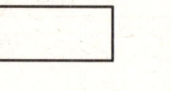 _____

11. 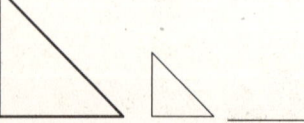 _____

12. 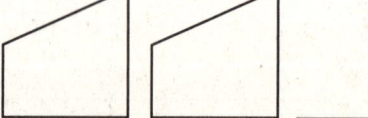 _____

13. 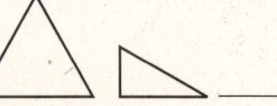 _____

14. 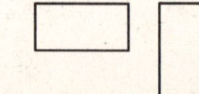 _____

Grade 4   78   Chapter 10

Name _____

11-1 Homework Practice

Customary Units of Length

Estimate. Then measure each to the nearest inch, $\frac{1}{2}$ inch, and $\frac{1}{4}$ inch.

1.

_____

2.

_____

3.

_____

4.

_____

What customary unit would you use to measure the following?

5. basketball _____

6. horse _____

Spiral Review

Write the number *B* best represents on each number line.

7.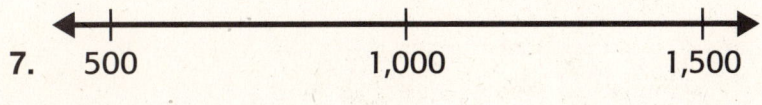

B = _____

8.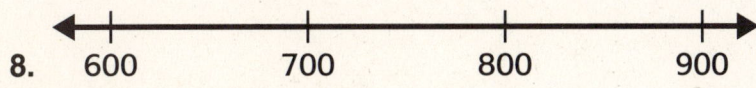

B = _____

Grade 4   Chapter 11

11-2

Name _____

Homework Practice

Convert Customary Units of Length

Convert.

1. 3 ft = _____ in.
2. 5 ft = _____ in.
3. 7 ft = _____ in.
4. 72 in. = _____ ft
5. 4 mi = _____ yd
6. 1 mi = _____ yd
7. 4 yd = _____ in.
8. 108 in. = _____ yd
9. _____ ft = 2 mi
10. _____ in. = 12 ft

11. Quiana lives 3 miles from school. Her friend Maggie lives 4,000 yards from school. Who lives closest to the school?

_____

12. The string on Abe's kite is 20 yards long. How many feet is the string?

_____

Spiral Review   List two items that would be about the same length as each measurement given. (Lesson 11-1)

13. 6 feet _____
14. 1 foot _____
15. 10 yards _____

Estimate. Then measure to the nearest inch, $\frac{1}{2}$ inch, and $\frac{1}{4}$ inch.

16.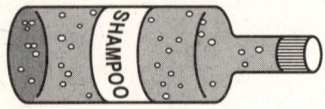

_____

Grade 4　　　　　　　　　　80　　　　　　　　　Chapter 11

11-3

Name _____

Homework Practice

Problem-Solving Strategy: Solve a Simpler Problem

Solve. Use the solve a simpler problem strategy.

1. Megan's family buys a roast chicken for $6, green beans for $2, mashed potatoes for $3, and milk for $2. How much did Megan's family pay for dinner? _____

2. Nicholas had to make 6 cakes for the party. Each cake takes 12 minutes to mix, 21 minutes to bake, and 27 minutes to cool and decorate. How long will it to make all 6 cakes? _____

3. Ricardo grows tomatoes in his garden. Each tomato plant yields 22 tomatoes each week. He has 5 tomato plants. How many tomatoes does he have after 4 weeks? _____

Spiral Review   Convert. (Lesson 11-2)

4. 36 in. = _____ ft

6. 2 mi = _____ yd

5. _____ in. = 2 yd

7. _____ ft = 3 mi

8. Holden is 49 inches tall. Sophia is 4 feet tall. Who is taller, Holden or Sophia?

_____

Name _____

11-4 Homework Practice

Metric Units of Length

Choose the best estimate.

1. Which is the best estimate for the length of a door?
   A. $1\frac{1}{2}$ kilometers   C. $1\frac{1}{2}$ centimeters
   B. $1\frac{1}{2}$ millimeters   D. $1\frac{1}{2}$ meters

   1. _____

2. Which is the best estimate for the length of a shoe?
   F. 30 meters   H. 30 kilometers
   G. 30 centimeters   J. 30 millimeters

   2. _____

3. What is the best estimate for the length of an eyelash?
   A. 4 centimeters   C. 4 millimeters
   B. 12 millimeters   D. 12 centimeters

   3. _____

4. Describe a situation when it would be appropriate to measure an object using centimeters. What about meters?

   _____

Spiral Review Solve. Use the solve a simpler problem strategy. (Lesson 11-3)

5. Maria found a store that sells handmade sweaters for $37. She wants to buy one for everyone in her family. She will buy 6 sweaters. How much will this cost? _____

6. James took a job delivering groceries in his neighborhood. He can carry 8 bags with each trip. If he takes 28 trips a day, how many bags does he deliver? _____

7. There are 32 students in Marissa's class. Each student started the year with 15 pencils. How many pencils did the class start with?

   _____

Grade 4

11-5

Name _____

Homework Practice

Measure Perimeter

Find the perimeter of each figure.

1. 8 ft / 8 ft / 8 ft / 8 ft (parallelogram)

   _____

2. 8 mm, 8 mm, 8 mm, 11 mm, 11 mm (pentagon)

   _____

3. 2 yd by 5 yd (rectangle)

   _____

Find the perimeter of each figure in units.

4. _____

5. _____

6. _____

Spiral Review   Choose the best estimate. (Lesson 11-4)

7. goldfish
   - A. 6 centimeters
   - B. 6 millimeters
   - C. 6 kilometers
   - D. 6 meters

   7. _____

8. bookshelf
   - F. 1 kilometer
   - G. 1 centimeter
   - H. 1 meter
   - J. 1 millimeter

   8. _____

Measure the object to the nearest centimeter.

9. _____

Grade 4   83   Chapter 11

11-6

Name _____

Homework Practice

Measure Area

Find the area of each figure.

1. 2. 6 mm ☐ 25 mm

Use the grid to draw each of the following squares or rectangles. Tell whether the figure is a *square* or *rectangle*. Then find the area.

3. Length: 6 units; width: 2 units:

4. Length: 4 units; width: 4 units:

Spiral Review — Find the perimeter of each figure. (Lesson 11-5)

4. 8 ft / 4 ft

5. 4 ft / 4 ft / 3 ft

6. 4 in. / 5 in. / 3 in. / 6 in.

7. 11 yd / 11 yd / 11 yd / 11 yd

8. 6 dm / 6 dm / 6 dm / 6 dm / 6 dm / 6 dm

9. 1 m / 5 m

Find the perimeter of each figure in units.

10. 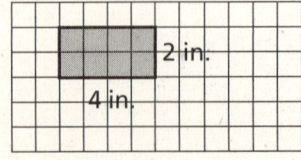 2 in. / 4 in.

11. 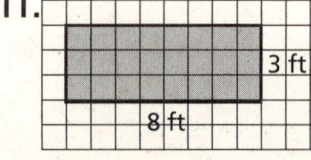 3 ft / 8 ft

Grade 4 — 84 — Chapter 11

Name _____

11-7

Homework Practice

Problem-Solving Investigation: Choose a Strategy

Use any strategy shown below to solve. Tell what strategy you used.

- Act it out
- Guess and check
- Look for a pattern
- Solve a simpler problem

1. A conference center has six rooms. Each room can hold up to 248 people. About how many people can fit in the conference center?

   _____

   Strategy: _____

2. Ryan's school is going on a field trip. If all six classrooms have 27 students going on the trip, how many students from the school are going? _____

   Strategy: _____

3. Cole has 26 trophies. Julia has eight more than Cole. Eric has seven more than Julia. How many trophies does Eric have?

   _____

   Strategy: _____

Spiral Review

Find the area of each figure. (Lesson 11-6)

4. 2 yd
   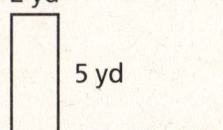
   5 yd
   _____

5.  _____

6. Mrs. Sanchez's room has an area of 1295 square feet. Her room is 35 feet long. How wide is her room? _____

7. Chelsea wants to know the area of the pool deck she scrubs. It is 25 feet. wide by 42 feet. long. What is the area? _____

Grade 4 — 85 — Chapter 11

Name _____

11-8 Problem-Solving Practice

Measure Temperature

Solve.

1. How would you dress for the day if you looked at the following thermometer before school? Hint: would you dress for cold weather or warm weather?

   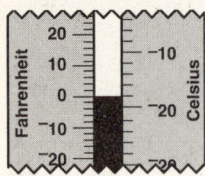

   _____

2. Michelle and Isaac each read a thermometer outside on a cool spring day. Michelle says it is 40°F outside. Isaac says it is 100°F outside. Who is correct? Explain your reasoning.

   _____
   _____

3. Is it more reasonable to say that a glass of cold water would be 40°F or 150°F? Explain.

   _____
   _____
   _____

4. Does the line on the thermometer go up or down when the temperature gets hotter? What about when the temperature gets colder?

   _____
   _____

5. The average June temperature in Mario's hometown is 75°F. Is this a cool temperature or a warm temperature?

   _____

6. Name two situations in which you might see a thermometer being used.

   _____
   _____

Grade 4   Chapter 11

Name _____

12-1 Homework Practice

Customary Units of Capacity

Choose the most reasonable estimate.

1.

   A. 1 fluid ounce
   B. 4 fluid ounces
   C. 1 cup
   D. 4 cups

2.

   F. 6 cups
   G. 60 cups
   H. 6 quarts
   J. 60 quarts

3.

   A. 2 fluid ounces
   B. 2 cups
   C. 2 quarts
   D. 2 gallons

4.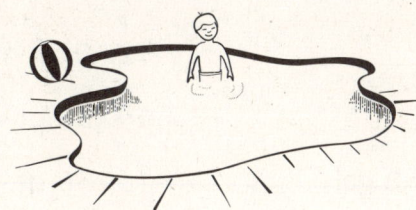

   F. 1,000 fluid ounces
   G. 1,000 cups
   H. 1,000 pints
   J. 1,000 gallons

1. ____
2. ____
3. ____
4. ____

5. Put the following units of capacity in order from largest to smallest.

   pint, fluid ounce, gallon, cup, quart

   _____

6. Name two things that would hold more than one gallon.

   _____

Spiral Review   Find the change in the temperature.
(Lesson 11-9)

7. 46°F to 7°F _____

8. 23°C to 100°C _____

9. 68°F to 171°F _____

10. 37°C to 2°C _____

Grade 4   87   Chapter 12

12-2

Name _____

Homework Practice
Converting Customary Capacity

Complete each conversion.

1. 4 pt = ☐ c _____
2. 6 qt = ☐ pt _____
3. 3 gal = ☐ qt _____
4. 3 c = ☐ fl oz _____
5. 40 fl oz = ☐ c _____
6. 16 c = ☐ pt _____
7. 2 gal = ☐ fl oz _____
8. 6 gal = ☐ qt _____
9. 28 qt = ☐ gal _____
10. 8 c = ☐ pt _____

Compare. Write >, <, or =.

11. 9 fl oz ◯ 1 c _____
12. 64 fl oz ◯ 8 c _____
13. 8 c ◯ 4 pt _____
14. 56 pt ◯ 24 qt _____
15. 1,152 fl oz ◯ 8 gal _____
16. 36 qt ◯ 9 gal _____
17. 5 qt ◯ 12 pt _____
18. 5 pt ◯ 8 c _____
19. 8 gal ◯ 50 qt _____
20. 5 pt ◯ 10 c _____

Spiral Review

Choose the most reasonable estimate. (Lesson 12-1)

21.

A. 1 pint
B. 5 pints
C. 1 gallon
D. 5 gallons

22.

F. 2 quarts
G. 4 quarts
H. 8 quarts
J. 20 quarts

21. _____

22. _____

Grade 4 — 88 — Chapter 12

12-3

Name _____

Homework Practice

Metric Units of Capacity

Solve. Use the act it out strategy.

1.

   200 mL   200 L

   _____

2.

   1 mL   1 L

   _____

3.

   3 mL   3 L

   _____

4.

   200 mL   200 L

   _____

5.

   5 mL   5 L

   _____

6. Identify 4 objects in the classroom that can hold more than one liter.

   _____

 Compare. Write >, <, or =. (Lesson 12-2)

7. 8 fl oz ◯ 1 c _____

8. 8 gal ◯ 30 qt _____

9. 5 pt ◯ 9 c _____

10. 12 qt ◯ 26 pt _____

11. 1,152 fl oz ◯ 9 gal _____

12. 12 pt ◯ 7 qt _____

Grade 4   89   Chapter 12

12-4

Name _____

Homework Practice

Customary Units of Weight

Choose the most reasonable estimate.

1.

   A. 5 ounces   **B.** 5 pounds   **C.** 50 pounds   **D.** 5 tons

   1. _____

2.

   F. 1 ounce   **G.** 10 ounces   **H.** 10 pound   **J.** 1 ton

   2. _____

3.

   A. 7 ounces   **B.** 7 pounds   **C.** 70 pounds   **D.** 7 tons

   3. _____

4. Ellie claims that her pet dog weighs 2 tons. Is Ellie's claim reasonable? Explain why or why not.

   _____

5. List two objects that weigh more than one ton.

   _____

Spiral Review Choose the more reasonable estimate.
(Lesson 11-3)

6. 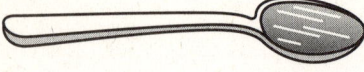   7.

   5 mL   5 L   4 mL   4 L

Name _____

12-5 Homework Practice

Problem-Solving Strategy: Choose a Strategy

Solve. Use logical reasoning.

1. Kristen, Josh, and Dan all play on soccer teams. One team is green, one is blue, and one is silver. Kristen's team is silver, and Dan's team is not green. What color team does each person play for?

   _____
   _____

2. Jasmine, Courtney, Taylor, and Inez are all on the same basketball team. Their jersey numbers are 4, 5, 8, 11. Inez's number equals the number of letters in her name. Jasmine's number is a two-digit number. Courtney's number is not a prime. What is Taylor's number? _____

3. Three labrador retrievers play at the park. One is yellow, one is black, and one is chocolate. Their names are Emma, Newton, and Sheldon. Sheldon is not yellow. The black dog's name is the shortest. What are the colors of each dog?

   _____
   _____
   _____

Spiral Review

Choose the most reasonable estimate of weight. (Lesson 12-4)

4.

5.

   A. 5 ounces   C. 50 ounces   F. 120 ounces   H. 12 pounds
   B. 5 pounds   D. 5 tons   G. 120 pounds   J. 120 tons

   4. _____
   5. _____

Name _____

12-6 Homework Practice

Convert Customary Units of Weight

Complete.

1. ☐ lb = 5 T 1,300 lb _____
2. 3 T 900 lb = ☐ lb _____
3. 5 lb 11 oz = ☐ oz _____
4. 14,000 lb = ☐ T _____
5. ☐ oz = 11 lb _____
6. 2 T = ☐ lb _____
7. ☐ oz = 1 lb 14 oz _____
8. ☐ T = 20,000 lb _____
9. 7 lb 5 oz = ☐ oz _____
10. 112 oz = ☐ lb _____
11. 9 lb = ☐ oz _____
12. ☐ T = 18,000 lb _____
13. 7 T 1,100 lb = ☐ lb _____
14. 48 oz = ☐ lb _____
15. 84 oz = ☐ lb ☐ oz _____

Spiral Review

Solve. Use logical reasoning. (Lesson 12-5)

16. Katherine watches the neighborhood children as they learn to ride their bikes. Some ride with training wheels, others do not. If there are 5 children riding their bikes, and there are 16 wheels, how many are riding with and without training wheels?

_____

_____

12-7 Homework Practice

Metric Units of Mass

Choose the more reasonable estimate.

1.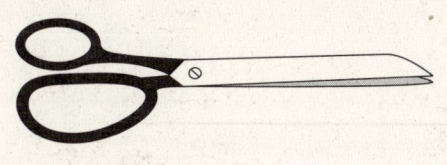

   20 g   20 kg

   _____

2.

   3 g   3 kg

   _____

3.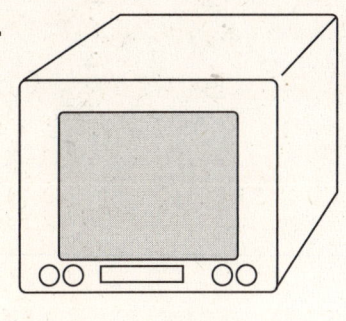

   20 g   20 kg

   _____

4.

   14 g   14 kg

   _____

5. The mass of a nickel is 5. What metric unit was used to measure the mass of the nickel?

   _____

6. The mass of a pen cap is 1. What metric unit was used to measure the mass of the pen cap?

   _____

Spiral Review   Complete. (Lesson 12-6)

7. ☐ lb = 3 T 1,200 lb _____

8. 2 T 700 lb = ☐ lb _____

9. 6 lb 12 oz = ☐ oz _____

10. 10,000 lb = ☐ T _____

Grade 4   93   Chapter 12

12-8

Name _____

Homework Practice

Estimate and Measure Volume

Find each volume.

1.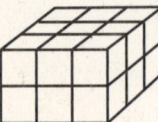

   cubic units _____

2.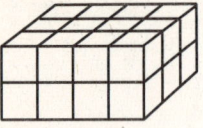

   cubic units _____

3.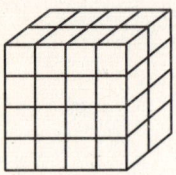

   cubic units _____

4.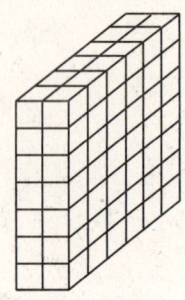

   cubic units _____

5.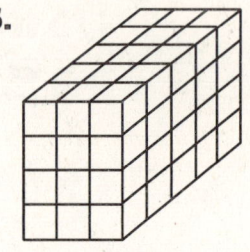

   cubic units _____

Estimate each volume.

6.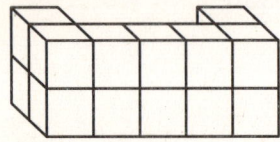

   cubic units _____

7.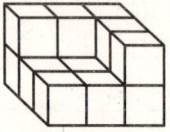

   cubic units _____

Spiral Review

Choose the more reasonable estimate. (Lesson 12-7)

8.

   10 g   10 kg

   _____

9.

   6 g   6 kg

   _____

Grade 4   94   Chapter 12

12-9

Name _____

Homework Practice

Problem-Solving Investigation: Choose a Strategy

Use any strategy shown below to solve. Tell what strategy you used.

- Act it out
- Guess and check
- Look for a pattern
- Work a simpler problem
- Use logical reasoning

1. For every day that everyone in class does his homework, Mrs. Ramirez puts two pebbles in a bowl. When she has 178 pebbles, the students will have no homework. How many days must everyone complete his homework before Mrs. Ramirez assigns no homework? _____

2. Alexis, Danielle, and Victoria each want to make a bracelet from beads. There are blue glass, purple plastic, and yellow clay beads. Alexis uses purple beads. Danielle prefers clay beads. What beads will each girl use? _____

Spiral Review

Find each volume. (Lesson 12-8)

3.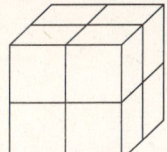
cubic units _____

4.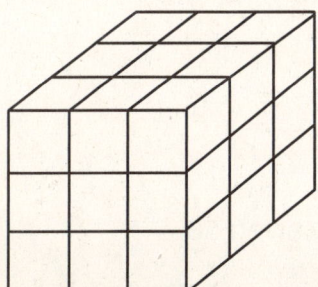
cubic units _____

5.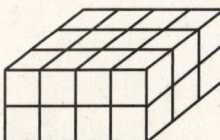
cubic units _____

Grade 4 — Chapter 12

12-10

Name _____

Homework Practice

Elapsed Time

The following are times of activities. How long is each activity?

1. Start: 6:15 End: 7:50 _____

2. Start: 4:45 End: 8:00 _____

3. Start: 10:10 End: 12:05 _____

4. Start: 3:30 End: 9:05 _____

Find each elapsed time.

5.

What time will it be in 45 minutes? _____

6.

What time will it be in 4 hours and 15 minutes? _____

7.

What time will it be in 9 hours and 10 minutes? _____

8.

What time will it be in 3 hours and 50 minutes? _____

Spiral Review

Solve. Tell what strategy you used. (Lesson 12-9)

9. Pumpkins cost $2 each. Erika paid the cashier $10 and received $6 in change. How many pumpkins did Erika buy?

_____

Grade 4   96   Chapter 12

15-2 Homework Practice

Estimate Decimal Sums and Differences

Estimate. Round to the nearest whole number.

1. 6.3
   + 4.6

2. 3.7
   + 5.4

3. 8.2
   + 12.6

4. 17.8
   + 11.1

Estimate by rounding to the nearest whole number. Then compare. Use >, <, or =.

5. 5.64 + 12.33 ◯ 14.62 + 8.18

6. 9.66 + 9.44 ◯ 13.71 + 5.32

7. 16.21 − 7.45 ◯ 18.83 − 9.13

8. 17.63 − 5.31 ◯ 15.45 − 6.74

9. Colin is 3.97 feet tall. Caroline is 3.15 feet tall. About how much taller is Colin than Caroline? _____

10. Ricardo has saved $23.46. Jasmine has saved $18.67. About how much more money has Ricardo saved than Jasmine? _____

Spiral Review

Round to the nearest whole number. (Lesson 15-1)

11. 3.26 _____
12. 18.48 _____
13. 73.33 _____
14. 7.77 _____
15. 53.61 _____
16. 88.86 _____

Round to the nearest tenth.

17. 2.13 _____
18. 19.34 _____
19. 57.53 _____
20. 6.76 _____
21. 33.46 _____
22. 88.68 _____

For exercises 23–24, round to the nearest whole number.

23. Jacob works 143.62 hours a year. Emma works 187.34 hours per year. About how many more hours per year does Emma work than Jacob? _____

24. Michelle's family is buying pizza for delivery. It will cost $23.74. About how much money will Michelle's family need? _____

15-3

Name _____

Homework Practice

Problem-Solving Strategy: Work Backward

Solve. Use the work backward strategy.

1. A number is divided by 4. Then 2 is added to the quotient. Finally the sum is multiplied by 3. The result is 12. What is the number?

   _____

2. Mrs. Washington can jog one mile in 9 minutes. She can walk one mile in 15 minutes. She always stretches for five minutes before exercising. She jogged 2 miles and walked 2 miles. If she finished at 9:15 A.M., what time did she start? _____

3. Alejandro has 4 times as many crayons as markers. He has 6 more markers than pencils. He has 12 pencils. How many crayons does he have? _____

4. Emily bought a $5 sandwich. She then repaid her friend $6. Now Emily has $8. How much money did she have originally? _____

Spiral Review

Estimate. Round to the nearest whole number. (Lesson 15-2)

5. 5.4

6. 2.8
   + 7.3

7. 9.3
   + 13.6

Estimate by rounding to the nearest whole number.

Then compare. Use >, <, or =.

8. 6.72 + 11.64 ◯ 13.33 + 9.44

9. 8.75 + 11.23 ◯ 14.16 + 5.89

10. 18.46 − 8.29 ◯ 14.95 − 5.26

11. Juan can throw a ball 23.47 yards. Michael can throw a ball 19.77 yards. About how much farther can Juan throw the ball than Michael? _____

12. Sydney can run a mile in 8.6 minutes. Melissa can run a mile in 7.4 minutes. About how much faster can Melissa run a mile than Sydney? _____

15-4

Name _____

Homework Practice

Add Decimals

Add. Use estimation to check for reasonableness.

1. 0.5
   + 0.3

2. 4.3
   + 5.42

3. $9.32
   + $4.98

4. 0.9
   + 0.7

5. 0.78
   + 8.56

6. $12.61
   + $ 6.50

7. 1.5
   + 0.7

8. 11.47
   +10.78

9. $13.01
   + $ 5.12

10. 42.31 + 8.77 _____

11. 6.4 + 4.2 + 2.7 _____

12. 52.89 + 48.24 _____

13. 4.2 + 3.33 + 8.1 _____

14. $46.75 + $17.17 _____

15. 7.1 + 2.54 + 3.48 _____

Spiral Review

Solve. Use the work backward strategy. (Lesson 15-3)

16. A number is multiplied by 4. Then 7 is subtracted from the product. Finally the result is divided by 3. The result is 7. What is the number?

    _____

17. Pedro took 15 minutes to walk home. He played basketball for 30 minutes. Then he ate a snack for 20 minutes. Finally he sat down to start his homework at 4:00 P.M. What time did he leave school?

    _____

18. Marissa has 5 times as many pairs of socks as DVDs. She has 4 more DVDs than computer games. She has half as many computer games as baseball caps. If she has 6 baseball caps, how many pairs of socks does she have? _____

15-5

Name _____

Homework Practice

Problem-Solving Investigation: Choose a Strategy

**Use any strategy shown below to solve.
Tell what strategy you used.**

- Work a simpler problem
- Use logical reasoning
- Draw a picture
- Make a model
- Work backward

1. Eric buys a ticket to the basketball game for $15. The bus fare to the game and home is $3.50. Snacks at the game cost $6.37. If Eric has $30, how much change will Eric have when he comes home? _____

   Strategy: _____

2. Drew spent 20 minutes completing his reading homework. He spent twice as long on science homework. He spent 10 minutes less on his math homework than he did on his science homework. How long did he spend on all of his homework?

   _____

   Strategy: _____

 (Lesson 15-4)

Add. Use estimation to check for reasonableness.

3. 0.4
   + 0.2
   -----

4. 1.8
   + 0.4
   -----

5. 0.56
   + 7.43
   ------

6. 0.8
   + 0.5
   -----

7. 3.7
   + 6.37
   ------

8. 13.28
   + 11.12
   ----

9. 39.62 + 7.24 _____

10. $37.53 + $18.64 _____

11. 53.71 + 33.87 _____

12. 5.3 + 3.8 + 1.9 _____

Grade 4   Chapter 15

15-6

Name _____

Homework Practice

Subtract Decimals

Subtract. Check your answer.

1.   3.6
    − 2.3

2.   8.22
    − 4.49

3.   19.65
    − 13.42

4.   4.2
    − 1.6

5. $8.15
    − $5.81

6. $21.07
    − $14.19

7.   5.4
    − 4.8

8.   12.32
    − 9.76

9.   41.26
    − 19.72

10.   6.9
    − 2.54

11. $15.76
    − $11.38

12. 55.55
    − 22.66

Spiral Review (Lesson 15-5)

Use any strategy shown below to solve.
Tell what strategy you used.

- Use logical reasoning
- Make a model
- Solve a simpler problem
- Draw a picture
- Work backward

13. Cody earns money selling lemonade. He earned $14.55 the first week, $11.75 the second week, $18.54 the last week. How much money did he make selling lemonade? _____

    Strategy: _____

14. Samantha has 15 packages of 12 plates. How many plates does she have? _____

    Strategy: _____